United States
Department of
Agriculture

Forest Service

Southern
Research Station

General Technical
Report SRS–137

Early Forestry Research in the South: A Personal History

Philip C. Wakeley

with illustrations and comments by
James P. Barnett

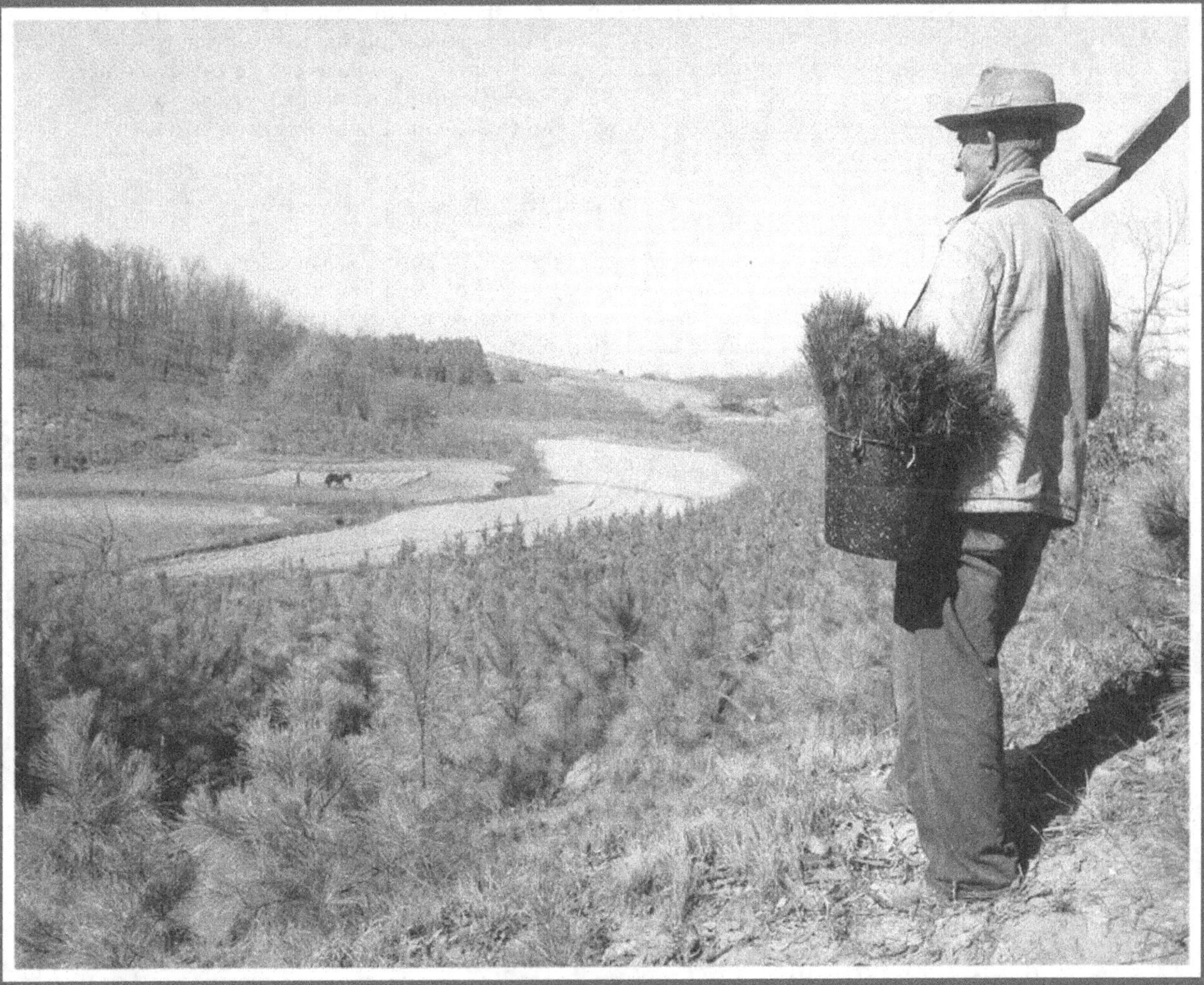

Authors:

Philip C. Wakeley, Deceased, Retired as a Research Forester in 1964 after working for 40 years for the USDA Forest Service, Southern Forest Experiment Station, in New Orleans, LA 70113; **James P. Barnett**, Retired Research Forester, USDA Forest Service, Southern Research Station in Pineville, LA 71360.

Cover:

This classic photo of the old man with a planting bar and a bucket of trees was the logo of Yazoo-Little Tallahatchie (Y-LT) Flood Prevention Project for 25 years (1948 to 1985). The Y-LT Project by the U.S. Department of Agriculture Forest Service was the largest tree-planting project (835,900 acres successfully reforested) that this country has known and was established to rehabilitate highly eroded lands in north Mississippi (Williston 1988). The Y-LT was a congressionally funded program which applied the reforestation and soil restoration technology developed by early Southern Forest Experiment Station scientists. The photo showing W.C. Turpin of Lafayette County, Mississippi, preparing to plant more trees while his brother plows in the valley, provides an outstanding example of good land use.

Photo credits:

Unless otherwise noted, the photos were from collections of the U.S. Forest Service, the Louisiana Forestry Commission (now Louisiana Office of Forestry), or the Louisiana Forestry Association. These organizations have extensive photo collections and many of the early photos were interchanged between organizations so that the identity of many of the original photographers has been lost. Professional photographers Elemore Morgan and Tommy Kohara took many of these photos. Sources for others are identified with the photograph.

Disclaimer

Pesticide Precautionary Statement

April 2011

Southern Research Station
200 W.T. Weaver Blvd.
Asheville, NC 28804

EARLY FORESTRY RESEARCH IN THE SOUTH:

A PERSONAL HISTORY

PHILIP C. WAKELEY

with illustrations and comments by

JAMES P. BARNETT

Abstract—Philip C. Wakeley, a pioneer research scientist for the U.S. Forest Service, Southern Forest Experiment Station in New Orleans, LA, began his career in 1924. He had an illustrious career with the Southern Station, and his research became the basis for the reforestation of the South's devastated forests. Upon his retirement in 1964, he presented the Station a personal overview of his early research, station programs, and personalities of many early scientists. Never before published, this history presents an intriguing look at the development of forestry research in the South from the eyes of one of the Southern Station's most prominent scientists.

Keywords: Forestry research, history of southern forestry, pine plantation management, reforestation of southern pines, seed and seedling physiology.

TABLE OF CONTENTS

FOREWORD

INTRODUCTION

The forests of the Southern United States were little influenced by man until the mid-19th century when they become the focus of an early export lumber business. Longleaf pine (*Pinus palustris* Mill.) was the choice species due to its straightness and self pruning that produced high quality lumber and high resin content that limited decay and insect attack. The South's original longleaf pine dominated forest is estimated at 90 million acres. As the supply of virgin stands began to decline in the Carolinas around 1860, harvesting gradually moved south and west and by the early 1900s was concentrated in the West Gulf Region. The introduction of railroad logging increased the efficiency to the point that insufficient longleaf trees remained uncut to provide for regeneration. Loblolly pine (*P. taeda* L.), a more aggressive seeder than longleaf, began to occupy what had been longleaf sites. But, loblolly regeneration lacks the fire resistance of longleaf and was easily destroyed on fire prone sites. Millions of acres of both upland and coastal plains were converted to agriculture, but much of those lands proved unsuited to such use and were soon abandoned. Both cutover and abandoned agricultural lands were considered open range and subjected to frequent burning and heavy grazing by cattle and hogs. These uses further complicated reforestation. The rebuilding of the South's southern pine forest was a major challenge as well as a major opportunity.

The Need for Management

The South initially depended upon European trained foresters to implement management and provide forestry training. George W. Vanderbilt early recognized the need for reforestation of his cutover land when he hired Gifford Pinchot in 1892 as a forester for his Biltmore Estate near Asheville, NC. When Dr. Carl Schenck replaced Gifford Pinchot in 1885, he established the Biltmore Forest School, which was one of the first scientifically, conducted forestry schools in this country.

This is a longleaf pine stand typical of those that occupied nearly 90 million acres of the lower Coastal Plain when European settlers arrived.

v

This land is typical of the cutover land in the West Gulf Coastal Plain Region. Harvesting was very complete in this western region and few seed trees remained to regenerate the longleaf pine forest. Many millions of acres of such land needed reforestation.

The need for forest management expanded quickly as the heavy harvest by lumber industries swept across the South. Northern investors came into the South in the late 1880s, purchased land inexpensively, and built mills for processing timber. For example, the Great Southern Lumber Company in Bogalusa, LA, ran four, 8-foot band saws that could produce 1 million board feet of lumber every 24 hours for more than two decades (Kerr 1958).

A survey of the South's forest resource in the early 1930s indicated that < 10 percent of the old-growth longleaf pine type remained and about 27 percent of the acreage had been clearcut without possible means of natural regeneration (table 1). It is also apparent that the longleaf forests in lower Coastal Plain topography had been more aggressively harvested and the proportion in clearcut conditions was over 37 percent. Here, too, the proportion with reproduction was less than for the more upland areas. This sample from the longleaf pine type by the Southern Forest Survey indicates the general condition of

the South's forest resources as a result of several decades of intensive harvesting (Wahlenberg 1946).

Wakeley (1954) stated that there were 13 million acres of forest land in need of planting. Later, Wahlenberg (1960) estimated that there were 29 million acres of idle land in need of reforestation. These conditions resulted from abusive agricultural practices that degraded soil productivity, coupled with exploitative timber harvesting without provision for regeneration.

Many lumber mill operators depleted the old-growth supply and moved to the Pacific Northwest, but a few far-sighted individuals began to work on a reforestation program that would provide for a continuing forest resource. Henry Hardtner, who became known as the "Father of Forestry in the South," established plots on the first reforestation "reserve" in 1913 in Urania, LA to support and guide pine reforestation (Wheeler 1963). Hardtner, as President of the Urania Lumber

Table 1—Distribution of forest conditions by topography within the longleaf pine type of the naval stores region in 1935 (adapted from Wahlenburg 1946)

Classification	Coastal Plain		Uplands		Total	
	acres	*percent*	*acres*	*percent*	*acres*	*percent*
Old growth	695,500	9.2	905,700	9.1	1,601,200	9.2
Second growth						
Sawlog size	960,100	12.7	1,545,200	15.6	2,505,300	14.3
Under sawlog size	2,434,100	32.2	4,302,600	43.5	6,736,700	38.2
Cutover with regeneration	642,500	8.5	1,173,200	11.8	1,815,700	10.4
Cutover with/out regeneration	2,819,600	37.3	1,974,200	20.0	4,793,800	27.5
Fire killed	7,600	0.1	1,700	<0.1	9,300	<0.1
Total	7,559,400	100.0	9,902,300	100.0	17,461,700	100.0

Henry Hardtner (left), President of the Urania Lumber Company and early advocate of reforestation.

Company, led an effort to create a State forestry organization in 1907. He placed 25,719 acres of his cutover forest land under a reforestation contract with the State of Louisiana with the belief that cutover lands offered long-term opportunities for profit (Maunder 1963). William G. Greeley, Chief Forester of the Forest Service, U.S. Department of Agriculture, remarked that even by 1920 neither foresters nor lumbermen had any real concept of the reproductive vigor of logged-over forests, or of how the growth rate was increasing as young trees replaced old

forests (Maunder 1963). In recognition of the problem, a Cut-Over Land Conference of the South was held in New Orleans, LA in 1917 that promoted the sensible use of cutover lands in which forestry, farming, and grazing all had a place in the economic use of forest lands.

Establishment of Research Programs

The need for forestry research was becoming apparent in 1915 when Samuel T. Dana of the Forest Service, in an endeavor to identify problems in need of study, established large research plots on Hardtner's reserve at Urania. In 1917, the Yale School of Forestry started sending its graduating classes to Urania, LA for 3 months of practical training. This program continued for several decades. Students under the direction of Professor H.H. Chapman established longleaf pine thinning and fire plots as well as other studies (Wheeler 1963). Early results of Chapman's Urania studies were summarized in publications such as "The recovery and growth of loblolly pine after suppression" (Chapman 1923) and "Factors determining natural regeneration of longleaf pine on cutover lands in LaSalle Parish, Louisiana" (Chapman 1926).

Prior to 1920 the knowledge and practice of forestry was limited in the South. W.W. Ashe (Ashe 1915), Austin Cary (White 1961), and W.P. Mattoon (Mattoon 1922) of the Forest Service traveled throughout the area, encouraging large landowners to practice forestry. Ashe, Cary, and Mattoon wrote a number of excellent bulletins on forest management.

In 1921, the Forest Service of the U.S. Department of Agriculture established the Southern and Appalachian Forest Experiment Stations at New Orleans, LA and Asheville, NC, respectively. The Southern Forest Experiment Station was

Yale forestry class of 1917 at Hardtner's spring camp location at Urania, LA. These spring camps lasted for about 3 months. H.H. Chapman and Henry Hardtner are seated on the second row from the left.

H.H. Chapman with his Yale University students established a number of research studies on Urania Lumber Company's land.

primarily responsible for research in the southern pine types (from South Carolina to east Texas) and the Appalachian Station for the mountain hardwood types. Initially each Research Station employed about a half dozen professional foresters who had to work under primitive conditions and with poor funding. A few other pioneering researchers joined the Research Stations in the mid-1920s, but little expansion of the program occurred until congressional passage of the McSweeney-McNary Forest Research Act of 1928. Thus began a general recognition of the need for forestry research efforts to deal with the multitude of problems resulting from

the thorough harvest of the native forests of the Southern United States.

WAKELEY'S PERSONAL HISTORY AND RESEARCH ACCOMPLISHMENTS

In 1924, the Southern Forest Experiment Station at New Orleans hired Philip C. Wakeley, recently graduated from Cornell University, the first 4-year school of forestry in the United States (Wakeley received a B.S. in 1923 and a M.F. in 1925). He was given the responsibility for conducting reforestation research. Phil Wakeley's research program was largely responsible for developing seed, seedling, and tree planting technology still in use today. His publication, "Planting the Southern Pines" (Wakeley 1954), with an earlier version (Wakeley 1935), served as the planting handbook for the Civilian Conservation Corps in the South and provided the information necessary to establish successful reforestation programs. "Planting the Southern Pines" is probably the most frequently cited forestry publication in the South and is still frequently cited although it has been out of print for many decades.

Wakeley also conducted early research related to genetics and tree improvement of the southern pines and was a charter member and chair of the Southern Forest Tree Improvement Committee. In 1929, he made the first controlled hybridization of southern pines, a cross of longleaf and slash (*P. elliottii* Engelm.). He established the first provenance test of southern pines. Planted in 1926-27 and remeasured at 15 years of age, loblolly pine from four different seed sources showed a striking difference in wood production (Wakeley 1944).

Austin Cary, a Forest Service forester from the Washington Office, spent winters in the South in the early 1910-1920s providing technical information to landowners. His death in 1936 was a serious loss to southern forestry.

Phil was a keen observer and keeper of meticulous records. Even after retirement, he could be called upon to provide specific locations to individual studies or trees in his genetics outplantings. His career covered 40 years, all with the Southern Forest Experiment Station in New Orleans, LA. He received the U.S. Department of Agriculture Superior Service Award, was elected a Society of American Foresters (SAF) Fellow, and was honored by the SAF with the Barrington Moore award for biological research in 1956. Phil is recognized across the South, as well as nationally and internationally, for his contributions to the restoration of southern forest ecosystems. During his career more than 100 publications of his studies were published, mostly on seed, nursery, and planting research, provenance tests, and hybridization of southern pines.

At his retirement in 1964, he presented the Station with a personal history of the early development of the Southern Forest Experiment Station. This document provides a fascinating insight to the establishment and development of forestry research in the South and the accomplishments made by the early cadre of forest researchers. The document entitled "A Biased History of the Southern Forest Experiment Station through Fiscal Year 1933" has never before been published.

Phil Wakeley at his retirement in October 1964. Dr. Carl Wenger, standing to Wakeley's left, was from the Washington Office.

Wakeley in his presentation to the Station did so with the caveat "I am giving the accompanying document to the Station with the following strings attached: It is to be typed "as is," without approval procedure or editing. All errors, other than typographic, are to be on my head."

When I was asked to make a historical presentation to the Southern Forest Science Conference at Atlanta in November 2001, I reread Wakeley's history and used it as a source document for my paper (Barnett 2004). It is such an interesting history that I believe it deserves to be published. Only poor photocopies of the document can be located, so it has almost been lost as a historical look at early research development in the South. As a young scientist, I had the pleasure of working and publishing with Phil a seed storage project (Wakeley and Barnett 1968). I have particular interest in and appreciation of Wakeley's work because much of my research career has focused on expanding and refining the reforestation technology initially developed by Wakeley.

Philip Wakeley in 1935, when conducting research at the Stuart Nursery in central Louisiana.

Since an original copy of this history cannot be located, there is no way to reproduce the photos that were used throughout the paper. Because Wakeley left a legacy of photographic material, I have tried to replace much of his original material with similar photos from the period and have added additional photos with captions to provide additional historical insight. To honor Wakeley's request, his text has not been edited and is presented as written.

JPB
Pineville, LA, March 15, 2010

A BIASED HISTORY
of the
SOUTHERN FOREST
EXPERIMENT STATION
through
FISCAL YEAR 1933

PHILIP C. WAKELEY

PREFACE

This is written during the sixth era of the Southern Station's history.

The various eras are fairly definite and distinct. They coincide only in part, however, with "administrations," either of Directors or of National political parties. Circumstances such as appropriations and war have overshadowed directorships, and more than one project worker has influenced Station events more than, and sometimes in spite of, his Director. What has given each era its distinctive character has been the ascendancy of certain attitudes and ideas.

Herein lies the difficulty of dating precisely the transition from one era to the next. The conceptions of ideas are rarely documented. Gestation periods are indeterminate. Times of birth may be lost among rival boasts of parentage.

> "Seven great cities all claimed Homer dead
> Through which the living Homer begged his bread,"

And the initiation of an idea that ushers in a new era tends to be similarly obscured as to date.

The six eras of the Southern Station, then, with their approximate durations appended for what they are worth, have been:

1. The primitive Era—1921-1928.
2. The Era of Expansion and Recognition—1928-1933.
3. The Relief Period (an era of very great expansion)—1933-1939.
4. The Defense Period and World War II—1939-1945.
5. The Era of Territorial Research—1945-1960.
6. The Present Era of "Renewed Functional Research in Depth—1960-

This is not the impressive volume that, for several years past, I have dreamed of writing.

I had planned to include all six eras of the Southern Station's history, with documented comments on such spicy subjects of bureaucratic idiocy, the publication problem, and the photographic morass. As I have written the following pages entirely on my own time, however, and as building a house in Ithaca and disposing of one in New Orleans have left me little time to spare, I have had to content myself with accounts of the Station's first two eras. And the writing is rough—little more than a first draft.

Individuals exist who know everything that has happened, is happening, and will ever happen at City Hall. I lack such insight and omniscience. Naiveté, then, and preoccupation with my own specialty, plus forgetfulness and a tendency to dramatize, combine to make this history a biased one. It is not only biased, but incomplete; a thousand pertinent facts remain scattered through official records that I have neither time nor inclination to review. Its individual items, ranging form verbatim excerpts from my diaries, through conversations reproduced from memory, to events "I seem to recall," are not equally dependable or precise. But it does re-create, as I saw them, the early days of the Southern Station I have known and loved and watched grow through more years than most Forest Service employees are vouchsafed on one assignment in one place.

PCW
New Orleans, Louisiana, October 23, 1964

THE SOUTHERN STATION IN 1924

When I reported for duty as a Temporary Field Assistant at the Southern Station on Thursday, October 16, 1924, about in the middle of the Primitive Era, there were fewer than twenty professionally trained foresters south of the Mason-Dixon Line and Washington, DC.

Nearly a third of these—Forbes, Hine, and Shivery in New Orleans, E.W. Hadley at Bogalusa, Louisiana, and Wyman at Starke, Florida—were on the Southern Station staff. Almost as many more—Frothingham, McCarthy, Korstian, and Haasis—constituted the staff of the Appalachian Station at Asheville.

State Foresters Besley of Maryland, Holmes of North Carolina, Sonderegger of Louisiana, and Siecke of Texas had forestry degrees. State foresters had not yet been appointed in the other Southern States. N.D. ("Don") Canterbury was employed at Crossett, H.C. Mitchell (later of "D+6" fame) had been hired as a forester by the Great Southern Lumber Company at Bogalusa, a few months before I arrived in New Orleans, and William L. Hall (who was a charter member of the Society of American Foresters) must also have been applying his profession in Arkansas.

I don't remember any others. I believe none of the then Supervisors of National Forests in the South had forestry degrees; typical of the times, they were "practical" men who had "come up through the ranks." Men like W.W. Ashe and W.R. Mattoon of the Forest Service and H.H. Chapman of Yale were, to be sure, doing invaluable work in the South, but as transients, not as permanent residents.

In 1924, what has since developed into the Southeastern Station was the Appalachian Station. To all practical purposes, the Appalachian's program and territory were limited to the mountain hardwood types. The Southern Station was responsible for research in the southern pine types. Its territory included the South Carolina and Georgia Coastal Plains and Georgia Piedmont; all of Florida, Alabama, Mississippi, and Louisiana; Texas as far west as the pine types went; and Arkansas south of the Arkansas River. In other words, Director Forbes and his permanent staff had between 1.4 and 2.0 States per man to cover, depending on how one scored fractions of States. Until 1928 or later, however, the Southern Station was effectively if informally enjoined from conducting federally financed research in the bottomland hardwood types within its territory.

Reginald D. Forbes (left) was State Forester of Louisiana prior to becoming the Director of the Southern Forest Experiment Station. He was Director from 1921 to 1927. W.R. (Billy) Hine (right) was the first forester on Forbes' staff, but resigned from the Station to become State Forester of Louisiana in 1925. Forbes graduated from Yale University and Hine from Cornell University.

Matty Mattoon provided forestry information to extension specialists across the South.

The Station's Program

By October 1924 the Southern Station had major duties or groups of studies under way in five general fields of research, and minor studies in a sixth.

In the field of mensuration the staff had, prior to my arrival, taken temporary sample plots in even-aged, second-growth stands throughout the South, and had nearly completed reduction of the data into "normal" volume, stand, and yield tables for unmanaged second-growth loblolly, longleaf, shortleaf, and slash pines. (I have always understood that Forbes assigned this undertaking its high priority; certainly he concurred in it. Donald Bruce of the Washington Office furnished technical guidance.) The last few plots were taken and the computations were completed in 1924–1925.

The tables were published in 1929 as Miscellaneous Publication 50 of the U.S. Department of Agriculture. They have been widely and severely criticized but even more widely used; in fact, they are still used, although so long out of print that copies are virtually museum pieces. They unquestionably contributed greatly to an understanding of the growth potentials of the four principal southern pines and to the first steps in practical forest management in the pine types. They have also inspired many later and more refined studies of growth and yield, but no equally comprehensive project in the mensuration of any southern species has been attempted.

In late 1924 studies of harvest and reproduction cuttings in longleaf pine were under way on two experimental areas—the "200-Acre Tract" (actually only 156 acres) at Bogalusa, Louisiana, and the "Tate Lease" of nearly 2 sections at McNeill, Mississippi. On the former, which has become part of the L.S.U. School of Forestry, the main point of interest was whether to leave 4 longleaf seed trees per acre ("minimum requirement") or 20 per acre ("desirable practice"). At McNeill, the interacting influences of cattle-grazing and fire upon the natural reproduction of longleaf pine, and of fire upon range capacity, were the main points at issue. The technical administration of these studies, with that of some others, had devolved upon Hadley a year or two before I joined the staff, and they remained under his charge until his resignation from the Service in 1926.

Miscellaneous Publication 50 (U.S. Department of Agriculture 1929) required extensive harvesting of study trees. This loblolly pine is being cut in Winn Parish, LA. MP 50 was reprinted in 1976 due to popular demand.

Off by himself at Starke, Florida, Lenthall Wyman, a modest, capable, humorous man, was conducting sensible empirical research in the production of gum naval stores. He had completed 2 years of experimental chipping on several hundred slash and longleaf pines by the fall of 1924, and one year's work on

Naval stores—the name derived from the early use of the resin for protecting wooden ships—were major forest products from early 1700s up until the 1970s. With the loss of old-growth longleaf pines, the industry rapidly declined after World War II.

several hundred more. Some of the planning of the work, though I don't know how much, had been done jointly by, or in consultation with, Austin Cary of the Washington Office and Dr. Eloise Gerry of the Forest Products Laboratory, but the solid research accomplishment was Wyman's.

Well before the end of the Primitive Era, Wyman's results had practically eliminated the No. 2 hack and the inch-wide, inch-deep streak throughout the Naval Stores Belt. They were replaced by the ½-inch by ½-inch streak made with a No. 0 hack, at a substantial saving in labor and in tree mortality, and with a considerable increase in the number of years a face or a tree could be worked. It took a big, powerful man to make the wide, deep streak with the No. 2 hack, and in the turpentine woods the chippers received the best pay. We used to speculate as to whether, by bringing about the adoption of the smaller hack that anyone could use, Wyman might not have reversed an evolutionary trend toward giantism among turpentine chippers.

Studies of thinning in even-aged, second-loblolly and shortleaf pine stands were concentrated at Urania, Louisiana, under W.R. (Billy) Hine, who had taken over some old plots established by Dana, Tillotson, and other men from Washington in 1912 and 1914, and had added some of this own. He also maintained there the famous Roberts Fire Plots in young longleaf pine.

Research on forest fire had loomed large since the Station's establishment in 1921. With the completion of the stand and yield tables, fire had become, officially, the most important project. Everybody worked at it.

There had originally been four Roberts Plots. The two that had been retained (each of ¼ acre, one burned annually and the other completely protected) and the McNeill Area (with each of these same two treatments applied to a 160-acre rectangle) might charitably be classified as experiments, though not very imaginative ones.

Photo taken at the Roberts' plots at Urania, LA in April 1940. From left to right: H.H. Chapman of Yale University; Station scientists C.W. Bickford, H.H. Muntz, C.W. Trayer, C.L. Forsling, Roy Chapman, T.R. Truax, John Curry, and J.M. Hughes; and Lloyd Blackwell, who was to become the Director of Louisiana Tech University's School of Forestry.

Photo of a burning study installed at Urania, LA in 1916 by W.R. Mattoon. On the right is a heavily burned site and on the left is a 5-year grass rough. Henry Hardtner of the Urania Lumber Company is on the right.

Most of the rest of the "research" on fire consisted of compiling horrifying lists of fire-killed seedlings, browned foliage on saplings, fire scars on living trees, and overgrown fire scars in freshly cut stumps. To lay out a permanent sample plot in a fresh burn was counted as a good deed. One of our Washington overhead laid out such a plot at Urania in 1925. When L.I. Barrett and I went to re-measure it 3 growing seasons later, we discovered that: (a) in tying the plot into the nearest permanent corner, our Washington superior had confused the north and south ends of the compass needle (which made the plot hard to find); and (b) he had neglected to establish an unburned check plot! (There were not replications, either, but nobody replicated in 1925, anyway.) H.H. Chapman did the Station an inestimable service when, during the Era of Expansion, he compelled us to abandon our evangelical attitude toward fire in favor of greater objectivity.

So much for the Station's five major lines of work during its fourth year. Its minor project was artificial reforestation, or "Forestation" (file designation "F") in the Service jargon of those days. Findings were as yet little in demand. The work was under Hadley's jurisdiction, as a sideline to the natural-reproduction, fire, and grazing study at McNeill and the methods-of-cutting study at Bogalusa. Unlike the much more extensive main lines of work, it was, for some reason never explained, broken down into subprojects—nursery, planting, and seed. (Perhaps the ease with which these could be designated Fn, Fp, and Fs had tempted higher authority beyond its strength.) Time spent on one or another of these subprojects had to be accounted to the nearest hour, and expenditures to the nearest penny, and reported at the end of each fiscal year. Why such minutely refined accounting was required of the least of the Station's projects and not the larger ones remains a mystery to this day, but the nuisance persisted until World War II.

By one of the greatest strokes of good fortune in my life, I was assigned to the Forestation Project. Another Temporary Field Assistant and I reported in New Orleans on the same day. He came in on the L&N Railroad, and I on the Southern. (I remember thinking in my innocence, that I was crossing the Mississippi when I crossed Lake Pontchartrain.) His train arrived in time for him to catch transportation to Urania, and was sent there to work with Hine. My later arrival resulted in my being sent up by the late afternoon train to Bogalusa to assist Hadley. Quite naturally and properly, Hadley used me mostly on the minor reforestation studies, where any mistakes I might make would do the least harm to the Station's program. The shaping of my whole professional career was as simple as that.

Forbes, Hine, and Shivery were in the field on October 16, 1924. It was the Station's first and, at the time, still its only clerk, Miss Very Spuhler (now Mrs. Ralph Lind) who welcomed me to the office with a straightforward cordiality that I still remember gratefully, introduced me to Station procedure, issued me an official-diary notebook (and, as I recall, a book of railroad scrip), explained the reason for my immediate assignment, and dispatched me to Bogalusa.

The Physical Plant

Station headquarters from 1921 until 1926 consisted of Room 323, Custom House. Although numbered, it was not properly a room, but the walled-off end of a corridor. It was fairly long, but narrow, with a single window at one end, in the immensely thick east wall of the building. (From that window, the following December, I observed the sun rising across the Mississippi from the Custom House. This astonished me, as I had learned by then I was on the Atlantic Ocean side of the River. That noon I checked out the Station's compass—as I recollect, we didn't get our second compass until 1925—and found, after a short walk and one quick sighting, that where the Mississippi passes the foot of Canal Street, it flows practically due north.) The window sill was less than a foot above floor level, and very broad. Room 326, to which we moved in 1926, had two windows with similar sills, on which we ran a number of the Station's sand-flat germination tests.

Room 323 contained Director Forbes' desk, Vera's typewriter desk and about three other desks, plus desk chairs, a few chairs for visitors and a bit of standard filing equipment. The filing equipment included one glassfronted bookcase section. In this section were four or five books (Hawley and Hawes' "Manual of Forestry for the New England States, Toumey's Seeding and Planting" and two or three others) and perhaps two dozen bulletins and pamphlets. This was the Station's entire library after 3-1/3 years. Staff members furnished their own references as, until October 1924, they had furnished their own automobiles. The week the Station acquired me as a field assistant; it also acquired its first two autos, Model T Ford-touring cars, complete with ill-fitting removable curtains. For at least the next 2 years, these were known, respectively, as Urania Ford and the Bogalusa Ford.

The natural-reproduction, fire, thinning and naval stores layouts at Bogalusa, McNeill, Urania, and Starke have already been mentioned. The corresponding facilities for Forestation research (into which I was plunged my first week at Bogalusa and which remained my absorbing and almost fulltime occupation for the next 27 years) consisted, in the fall of 1924, of ten 4- by 12-foot seedbeds and an acre of plantations at McNeill, another ten 4- by 12-foot seedbeds and 4 acres of plantations at Bogalusa and six or seven incompletely labeled sacks and jars of 1923 pine seed.

Each nursery bed contained 24 drills of seedlings. Each unit of six drills, and in some instances each individual drill, was covered by a separate "working plan" often returned to the Station for two or three rewritings before final approval by the Washington office. Harper annexed the entire file of these absurd "plans" when he became the Station's first Forest Management Division Chief in 1935 and used them with deadly effect in his battle to introduce the type of study plan we write today.

In 1922, this nursery was established by the Great Southern Lumber Company at Bogalusa. It reportedly was the first of its kind in the nation.

Casual visitors had poked most of the keys and none of the type bars the keys had raised had dropped down again. Hadley said, "Clean it!" I dared not take it apart but swabbed and trickled kerosene through it for most of 2 days and made it work. Indeed, it served the Bogalusa office well until it was transferred to another work center during the Civilian Conservation Corps (CCC) period.

This unromantic introduction to forest research was alleviated a little by checking of some computations with Hadley and by a bit of work on an experimental cone kiln in his back yard on Memphis Street. The kiln, knocked together of cheap lumber, was slightly larger than an up-ended desk and was

Among all the treatments in all the Forestation and other experiments laid out at the Station up to and including the fall of 1924, not a single one was replicated. The first replication was made accidentally in 1925, when an extra 3-foot segment of one of the Bogalusa seedbeds was sown as a second untreated check against a series of chemical-weeding experiments. This proved to be a most embarrassing replication. Compared with the first check, all the chemical-weeding treatments had favorable effects on the pine seedlings. Compared with the second check, all the treatments were adverse. As the two untreated checks lay about 50 feet apart, with all the unreplicated chemical treatments sandwiched in between them, the simplest explanation seems to have been that the checks were at the opposite ends of a soil-fertility gradient.

MY OWN EARLY WORK

My first task at Bogalusa had nothing to do with trees. It was to clean the typewriter.

The typewriter was an unused Underwood obtained "from surplus," as we say nowadays. It had been in possession of the Army from sometime during World War I until late 1923 or thereabouts and was understood to have been stored on the ground under a tarp. Be that as it may, the last decaying fragments of its wooden box had fallen off when it arrived at Bogalusa about a year before I did. Its thick coat of grease had saved it from rust but had retained generous amounts of gritty dust blown in from the gravel street below our second floor office in the old Washington Bank and Trust Company building.

Phil Wakeley observing the growth of longleaf pine. He was a devoted advocate of longleaf.

uncontrollably heated by a flat, 2-burner oil stove, which smoked prodigiously.

My personal diary for Tuesday, October 21, 1924, reads:

> ... *A day of quiet adventure. Did my first real field work, classifying and tallying loblolly seedlings in the "spacing experiment." Saw my first buzzard and my first lizard and drove my first Ford.*

I might have added "or any other car," as I had never had a chance to drive before this time. I might also have added "and got my first redbug bites." It had not yet become standard Station procedure to warn northern-born and trained personnel of the existence of chiggers, and I had innocently sat on the ground to eat my lunch. I did not discover the resulting welts; however, until after I had written my diary and undressed for bed.

The "spacing experiment" I started re-measuring that day was the loblolly plantation, containing an acre apiece at 5- by 5-, 6- by 6-, 6- by 8-, and 8- by 8-foot spacing, that the Station had established in 1922-23 in Section 17 of the Great Southern Lumber Company's "1,200 Acre Tract" southwest of Bogalusa. The tract was actually only 805 acres in area but in those days the Company, with an eye to publicity, rounded off all constructive undertakings to the next higher 100 or 1,000 acres and fires to the next lower 100 or 1,000. Thanks to our early remeasurements and to the Company's constant cherishing through two reorganizations and changes in ownership, the spacing experiment is still a useful asset of the Institute of Genetics.

My "tally," made when the trees were 2 years in plantation and 3 from seed, was the first in any of our experimental plantations at Bogalusa. Hadley had me measure the heights in inches because we had a Biltmore stick with an inch scale on it. Neither he nor I realized how soon the growth of southern pines would outmode the inch as a unit of measurement. In blind adherence to the principle of consistency, we continued to measure these and all later Bogalusa plantation heights in inches till slash, loblolly and shortleaf trees were 5 years and longleaf trees were 9 years in plantation and maximum heights approached or exceeded 20 feet. In reworking the field data, as we continue to do with punched cards in some of our genetics studies, we have to remember to divide the first few fields by 12 to reduce mean heights to feet. Beginning with the loblolly spacing "tally" on October 21, my work rapidly became more varied, more interesting and more nearly what I had expected forest research to be like. In fact, I was entranced with it. In the brief period of 2 weeks, I measured and described planted trees, transcribed "data" (I forget just what and my diary doesn't specify), extracted and weighed seed (1924 was locally a good seed year and longleaf, loblolly and shortleaf cones were mature) and went to New Orleans to meet Director Forbes and to work on curves and maps. I made out my first expense account, too—actual expenses, not per diem and with a subvoucher to support each item in

This sign designated an experimental nursery established in conjunction with the Great Southern Lumber Company, an important cooperator with the Southern Forest Experiment Station during the 1920s and early 1930s.

excess of a dollar—and swore—to it before a duly constituted official. We could swear to accounts before notaries at 50 cents per oath or swear free before smalltown postmasters, but as I recall, some venerable Civil Servant in the Custom House witnessed my first account, without charge.

Employment Status

All this time, however, I was in great perturbation of spirit regarding both my professional career and my livelihood. I had been on the Junior Forester Register but in late summer had refused a job managing the West Point Military Academy woodlot. Even though the job had paid only two-thirds the minimum salary for which the Register qualified me, my refusal counted as one of the three allowed me. My acceptance of my current Field Assistant job exhausted a second choice, even though the appointment was temporary. Would I get a third offer? Would it be for a permanent job and in research, or might I, in 2 or 3 months, be without work? Chris, Mrs. Wakeley, was working in Ithaca, but we didn't know whether or not she was pregnant (at least I didn't know because while I had been sent to Bogalusa, all my mail had been sent to Urania) and our bank account was very low.

On October 31, 1924, I received notice that I was still on the Junior Forester Register.

On November 4, I received a tentative offer of permanent appointment as Junior Forester on timber sales on the Whitman National Forest in Oregon, which I accepted by wire on November 5 (with regrets to Forbes) and which was confirmed on November 6. (Chris wired me enough money for a oneway ticket west.) On the sixth also, I received mail and learned that she wasn't pregnant and on November 7, Forbes phoned me long distance from New Orleans—itself a noteworthy event in view of the Station's budget—that I had been given a permanent appointment as Junior Forester at the Southern Station, effective November 10. With characteristic

This photo was taken on the J.K. Johnson Tract of the Palustris Experimental Forest in April 1940. At the left rear is a longleaf plantation spacing study planted in 1934-1935 that was controlled burned in January 1938. This study continues today and is providing significant information on the growth and yield of managed longleaf pine plantations. On the right rear is a slash pine spacing study planted at the same time that was destroyed during World War II when limited resources were lacking to protect the area from fire and animal damage. From left to right are Station scientists: T.R. Truax, G.W. Tayer, C.L. Forsling, H.H. Muntz, J. Curry, P.C. Wakeley, and C.L. Bickford. The photo is by Station Director E.L. Demmon.

consideration for his staff, he had got me transferred from the Whitman to the Southern Station in time to save me the cost of the round trip to Oregon. He told me later that he had chosen me in preference to a rival bachelor candidate because he considered married men steadier. I have been at the Southern Station ever since.

Chris joined me in New Orleans the morning of Sunday, November 30, with the last of our meager funds and we returned that night to my room in Mrs. McRae's boarding house at 310 Mississippi Avenue. It probably was the coldest house in Bogalusa, but we didn't care. We were together again and I had my job in research. I signed the oath of office before the Bogalusa postmaster November 25 and resigned it before him (I forget from what necessity) on December 13, 1924 at the age of 22.

Both my recollections of and my notes on the four years following my permanent appointment are so vivid and cover such varied subjects, that they threaten to overshadow all the years from 1928 on. It is with events as it is with trees. During the CCC period, I directed the planting of three quarters of a million trees on the J.K. Johnson Tract near Alexandria, and today, I can identify only one of these trees without a map. At Bogalusa, where I planted a mere 18,000 or 19,000 with my own hands, I can walk straight to and identify a hundred distinctive individuals at will, despite the

greater lapse of time since planting. Yet the Johnson Tract plantations, like the later years of work, were in general far more productive. A sense of proportion therefore limits me to just enough episodes to show how primitive the Primitive Era really was.

EXAMPLES OF PRIMITIVE RESEARCH

Experimental Plantations at Bogalusa

The Coburn's Creek and Upper Coburn's Creek Experimental Plantations, 3.8 and 4.1 miles westnorthwest of Bogalusa on the highway to Franklinton, are a good example of our research at this stage of the Station's development.

Hadley and I laid out 12 acres at Coburn's Creek just after my permanent appointment, and we started planting on December 13, 1924. We had foresight enough to put the slash pine next to the creek and the longleaf on the slope, with the loblolly in between. The effects of the severe drought of 1924; however, combined with our abysmal ignorance of subordinate vegetation (even of pitcher plants) led us to put part of the loblolly and nearly all the slash 6- by 6-foot spacing on a poorly drained "crawfish" site and everything else on well drained soil. This oversight alone vitiated about a third of our planting experiments.

The six 1-acre plots in the slash and longleaf pine spacing experiments were all right, except that spacings were not replicated and that we spaced the slash 5 by 5, 6 by 6 and 8 by 8 feet and the longleaf 6 by 6, 8 by 8 and 10 by 10. We should have reversed these assignments of spacings to species. Enough was known of the growth habits of the two, even in 1924, to suggest that slash would stagnate at the closer spacings, whereas longleaf would differentiate its crowns well.

The other comparisons we made in the Coburn's-Creek Plantations were, with one exception, footling in the extreme. We compared "fall" (December) with "spring" (February) planting; "mattock" with "dibble" planting; and "pruned" (6-inch) with "unpruned" (18- to 30-inch) roots. The "dibble" was the old Great Southern planting bar originally suggested to Red Bateman by Austin Cary and greatgrandfather of the modern Council Tool Company's planting bar.

These tests of season, tool and root pruning were laid out with slash, loblolly and longleaf in half-acre plots at 6- by 8-foot spacing—that is, with 12 rows of (plus or minus) 33 trees each, per half-acre. In each half-acre, the treatments to be contrasted were planted in alternate rows. Essentially, half of all the trees planted, other than those in the spacing plantations, were "untreated checks," as they were rootpruned seedlings of acceptable size, barplanted during the normal winter planting season. There were no factorial combinations of treatments. And, so far as method of planting was concerned, *all* the trees in the spacing plantations were untreated checks. Small wonder that we never got any large or consistent differences among these treatments in survival or early growth, either here or at Upper Coburn's Creek, where Tom Barron, Roy Chapman and I established "seasonal repeats" the following year. Seasonal repeats, that is, of all except the comparison of unpruned with pruned roots of longleaf pine. We gave that up. It cost too much to drive the planting bar 20 or more inches into the stiff clay subsoil and poke the unpruned roots into the slit with a forked stick.

The one comparison that paid off was of seedling grades. In 1924, we had an acre and a half unassigned to treatments at Coburn's Creek. Hadley said, "Think of something." I remembered a spruce seedling-grade exercise under Professor Samuel N. Spring at Cornell and set up some grades, purely by eye, in the available slash and loblolly stock. I was not yet up to formulating grades for longleaf seedlings which still looked like grass to me. In both survival and growth, the grades planted at Coburn's Creek in 1924-25 and "repeated" at Upper Coburn's in 1925-26 differed consistently and to an economically important extent, for both species in both years.

This seedling grading experiment was my first technical contribution at the Southern Station. Very directly it laid the foundation of the system of "morphological grades" that I first published in U.S. Department Agriculture Tech. Bul. 492 in

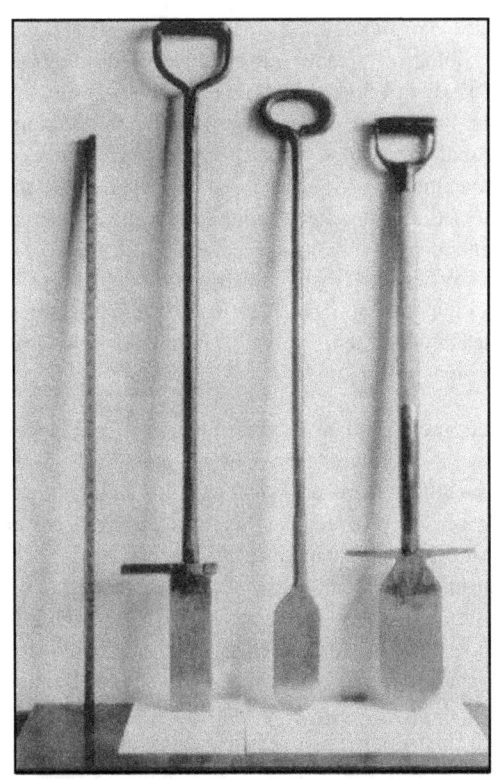

Early versions of the planting bar or "dibble." The handle of the one on the left was modified and became the standard hand-planting tool of the South.

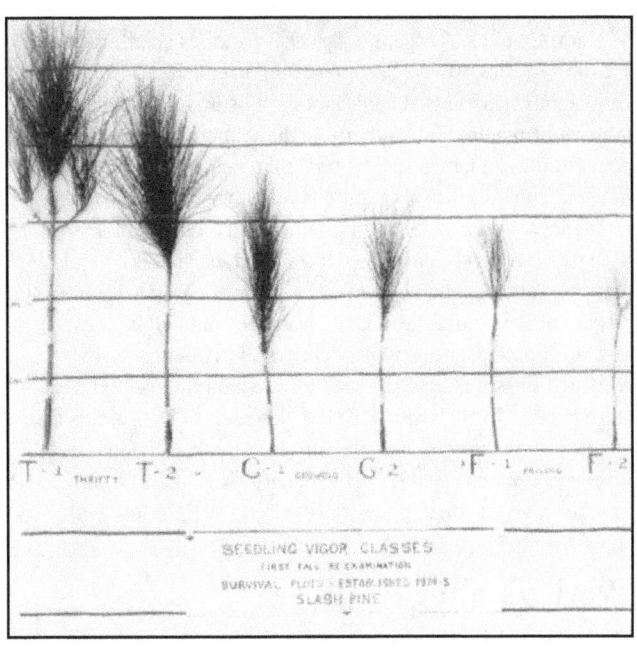

Wakeley's research on seedling grades began at the Bogalusa location, but it was refined and upgraded when he worked at the Stuart Nursery in Central Louisiana and conducted outplanting trials on the J.K. Johnson Tract of the Palustris Experimental Forest. Wakeley worked with the Civilian Conservation Corps at the nursery and outplanted nearly ¾ million trees in studies on the Experimental Forest. His work was so comprehensive that his morphological seedling grades for bareroot stock (Wakeley 1954) are still used today.

1935. These morphological grades sometimes fail to coincide with "physiological" grades (later dubbed "physiological qualities"), which I first attempted to define at the 1948 meeting of the Society of American Foresters in Boston and which actually determine capacity to survive. Because of such failures to coincide, various agencies have culled millions of plantable seedlings and have planted millions that should have been culled. Yet the morphological grades are the only kind it has yet proved feasible to apply in the nursery bed, in the packing shed or at the planting site and they are still used, much as I set them up in 1924, almost everywhere that southern pines are planted.

We re-examined the planted trees at Coburn's and Upper Coburn's Creek each year for the first 5 years in the field—the longleaf seedlings, because of their slow initial height growth, for the first 9. We recorded heights (in *inches*, as mentioned earlier), vigor (rather subjectively and, as it turned out, to no useful purpose) and all injuries we could identify. Map wise notes on letter size sheets enabled us to identify each individual tree, as indeed, we can still do. Shivery, who had come to the Station from 2 years' soils survey work in the old Bureau of Soils, made us an excellent soils map of the Coburn's Creek Area, with the help of which Roy Chapman and I acceptably mapped the soils in the nearby Upper Coburn's Creek Plantations. The map wise notes served a good purpose in connection with soil types, too, as we were able to mark the soil type boundaries between individual trees in the field notes.

The upshot was this. Having set out to learn all about seasons of planting, tools, rootpruning, spacing and (as an afterthought) seedling grades, we learned something useful about grades, little about spacing that could not have been deduced from general principles and virtually nothing about seasons, tools or root-pruning. Thanks to Shivery's soils map; however, we did get some insight into species-soils relationships and thanks to meticulous annual re-examinations, with records kept separate by individual trees, we learned a tremendous amount about ice-damage, rabbit-damage, Nantucket tip moth, brown-spot needle disease of longleaf pine and that plague of planted loblolly and slash pines, southern fusiform rust. Fortunately also, we recorded the sources of the seed from which the planted trees were grown. In the present Era of Research in Depth, this fact, coupled with the complete file of notes on the individual trees, gives the Coburn's and Upper Coburn's Creek Plantations unique value for forest genetics research.

Work Trading

During the Primitive Era and even through part of the Era of Expansion and Recognition, there were about as many lines of work underway as there were permanent members of the staff. We had a few temporary field assistants but only a few. Much of the work required pairs of men or small crews. Until the lush days of the New Deal; therefore, work trading was a feature of the Station's program.

Caroline Dormon, educator, artist, and conservationist, led the effort to establish a National Forest in Louisiana. She met with Col. Greeley, then Chief Forester, and he sent W.W. Ashe to meet with Miss Dormon. Ashe and others, such as Wakeley, provided information needed for the State Legislature to pass an enabling act. She met with Henry Hardtner, then State Senator, to prepare an omnibus forestry bill. Ashe stated, "Miss Dormon was the first and most persistent worker for the National Forests in Louisiana." For this and her long-term work in forestry education, she became the first female member of the Society of American Foresters.

Such work trading varied my assignment to artificial reforestation by taking me to McNeill in January 1925 to count longleaf seedlings on 1/100-acre "quadrats"—actually 6.6- by 6.6-foot plots. In the spring of that year, it engaged me at Bogalusa, Louisiana, Laurel and Meridian, Mississippi; in eastern Texas, at Sylacauga, Alabama and clear to New Bern, North Carolina on the so-called "Extensive Survey." From May through July 1925 and for a briefer period in 1926, it took me to Starke, Florida to work with Wyman on naval stores; to Rusk and Maydelle, Texas in April 1926 during a heavy discharge of shortleaf pine pollen to lay out fire plots with Demmon; to Camp Pinchot, Florida, on the old Choctawhatchee National Forest (now Eglin Field) to help initiate the sandhill studies that were abandoned in 1931 and revived (a few days after we had thrown away the old files!) with the establishment of our present Marianna Project.

In mid-August 1926, I drove the car for W.W. Ashe when he made the reconnaissance that led to the purchase of the Kisatchie National Forest; in 3 days, on what is now the well stocked Red Dirt Area, we found and photographed as a curiosity, a single small patch of longleaf pine seedlings.

I represented the Station at the Forest Products Laboratory Program Conference at Madison in 1929 and from the fall of 1926 until Dr. Thomas E. Snyder's arrival on July l, 1934, I handled all the Station's entomological specimens and correspondence. In fact, practically the only thing I did not work on was hardwoods.

The 200-Acre Tract

Even before my permanent appointment in November 1924, my seed, nursery and plantation measurements began to be interlarded with computations for the longleaf methods-of-cutting study on the 200-Acre Tract at Bogalusa.

The tract, now included in the L.S.U. Forest School forest, lies between Bogue Luce and Thompson Creek, about 10 miles west-northwest of Bogalusa, on the highway to Franklinton. (In the late Twenties, the natural range of slash pine extended northwest to Bogue Luce but not to Thompson Creek. By now; however, though I have not had occasion to check, natural reproduction of slash, from native parents, may have occurred at or beyond Thompson Creek.) Calling the area the "200"-Acre Tract was an example of the Great Southern Lumber Company's cheerful roundingoff to the next higher hundred; the actual area, if I remember correctly, was 156 acres. In a characteristically cooperative spirit, the Company had leased the tract to the Station for a dollar a year and had undertaken to log it in any manner desired for research. The Station had laid out a "minimum requirements" and a "desirable practice" block north of the highway and a similar pair of blocks south of it, with many 1/100-acre "quadrats" (6.6- by 6.6-rectangles) on which longleaf seedlings were to be counted. I forget how fencing of the area was financed but almost certainly it was not from federally appropriated funds.

My part in the establishment of the study was to plot on the area base map the block corners, "quadrats" and all the longleaf seed trees left on and near the four methods-of-cutting blocks. Hadley, Shivery, John Byrne and perhaps one or two others had worked for weeks tying in these corners and trees with transit and tape measurements. Bearings had been disregarded; ties were by 2 angles and included side, 2 sides and included angle or 3 sides of a triangle, to permit calculations of latitudes and departures. The third of these three methods, although it involved the most difficult calculations, had been used freely. I had to send to Ithaca for trigonometric tables for the work, as the Station had none.

This study on the 200-Acre Tract tells volumes about the state of forest research in the mid-Twenties, both in the Service in general and at the Southern Station in particular.

It was not out of order to use transit and tape to traverse the boundary of the tract and to lay out one or two base lines from which to locate interior points. For all the interior block corners, "quadrats" and individual longleaf seed trees, compass bearings and taped distances would have been amply accurate and far cheaper in terms of both field time and office time. Using the transit for these was nothing but the symptom of a yearning to be "scientifically accurate."

W.W. Ashe, a noted botanist, led Forest Service efforts to purchase land for National Forests across the South. The Ashe Nursery at Brooklyn, MS was named in his honor.

Mark Lehrbas laying out a research plot related to the first forest survey in 1931.

On what kind of an experiment was this scientific precision lavished?

In the first place, it was hardly an experiment. It was the considered opinion of the staff that both the "minimum requirement" (4 longleaf seed trees per acre) and the "desirable practice" (20 seed trees per acre) would insure adequate reproduction. In spirit, the undertaking was really to "demonstrate" that 20 trees would restock the ground more abundantly and would also constitute a residual stand capable of financing a second cut and hence, would be better business in the long run.

Second, the "upper" and "lower" pairs of blocks were not intended to be and were not in fact, replications in the statistical sense, to provide an error term. They were designedly put in on soils and in stands as different as possible from each other (a fine example of confounding), to "demonstrate" (again!) that the arbitrarily specified methods of cutting would work anywhere.

Third, although infinite care was used in locating "quadrat" corners with transit and steel tape, no such care was used in selecting the longleaf pines to be left as seed trees. The Great Southern Lumber Company set a date for logging the area in connection with their regular operation on surrounding land. Unaware as yet of the ponderousness of federal operations, they kept the date. A voluminous correspondence about the study was still in progress between New Orleans and Washington, when in desperation, Hadley went out and marked the trees to be left. As he said in his establishment report: "The marking had to be done hurriedly to keep ahead of the saws."

But the hasty marking was not the worst. The chief flaw in the study was that, instead of being laid out on typical longleaf sites on upper Coastal Plain slopes or ridges, it was laid out on diverse but generally fertile soils in the forks of a creek, where only centuries of frequent burning had kept longleaf ascendant over loblolly, shortleaf and hardwoods. Ecologically, it was the last place where a longleaf reproduction study should have been put.

The outcome? Despite good longleaf seed crops in 1924, 1927, 1928 and 1932, only 26 longleaf seedlings, as I recall, ever became established on the acre or so of observation "quadrats." Under the complete protection from fire that the Station specified and the Company achieved, these longleaf seedlings were all suppressed and killed by loblolly and shortleaf that seeded in from trees along the breaks or by hardwood brush. Meanwhile, from the same 1924, 1927, 1928 and 1932 seed crops, F.O. ("Red") Bateman, Head Ranger of the Great Southern Lumber Company, without resorting to tape, transit or "quadrats" successfully reproduced longleaf on 45,000 acres of the Company's land. Alas for the Station's ultra-scientific research!

Red Bateman

This is as good a point as any to pay a long overdue tribute to F.O. ("Red") Bateman. His nickname, by the way, derived from his fiery countenance, not from his hair, which was brown.

Unlike his younger brother, Bryant Bateman, of the L.S.U. Forest School faculty, who took his doctorate at Ann Arbor, Red was not professionally trained. My impression is that he must have graduated from high school about 1913 and gone to work in the woods for the Great Southern Lumber Company right afterwards. Whatever the chronology of earlier events, he had sufficiently made his mark by 1919-20, when the Company's serious forestry program began, to be appointed Head Ranger and he proved to be one of the greatest silviculturists the South has known. Thousands of acres of Crown Zellerbach's second-growth longleaf at Bogalusa, all the Company's pine plantations and, in a very real sense, most of the pine plantations in the South, stand as a monument to his genius. For many years all the rest of us merely followed or wrote up what he developed and showed us.

From the start of the Company's artificial reforestation at Bogalusa in 1919-20, he was the prime mover in developing planting principles and techniques. By 1922-23, two growing seasons before I arrived at the Station, he had worked out the

F.O. "Red" Bateman was Head Ranger for the Great Southern Lumber Company and contributed greatly in developing reforestation technology for the southern pines.

essentials of the general practice still employed today—slit planting of bare-rooted 1-0 stock grown without shade in the nursery. The 6- by 8-foot spacing he chose as most suitable and economical for southern pines was the almost universal standard throughout the South for many years and few drastic departures from it seem justifiable even now.

Red's first big silvicultural crop was in 1920-21. He sensed the import of the unprecedentedly heavy 1920 seedfall on 10,000 acres being logged or about to be logged in what later became known as the "South Pasture" at Bogalusa and personally persuaded Colonel Sullivan, then General Manager of the Great Southern Lumber Company, to let him fence the entire area against hogs. No finer stand of pole-size longleaf than that inside Red's fence line exists today. Outside, before the seedlings were out of the grass—see figure 39 of the U.S. Department Agriculture Agriculture Monograph 18—hogs had reduced the original catch of thousands per acre to two or three seedlings per acre.

By 1923, Red had nursery and planting techniques for loblolly and slash pines pretty well under control. That spring, V.H. Sonderegger, who had succeeded Forbes as State Forester of Louisiana in 1921, gave the Great Southern Lumber Company half a pound of longleaf pine seed—geographic source not noted. Just out of curiosity, J.K. Johnson, who filled the position of Company Forester, had Red sow the seed in the Company nursery. Both he and Red wanted to watch pine seedlings develop. At lifting time, in the winter of 1923-24, J.K. told Red to dig up the 500 or so longleaf seedlings and throw them away. Red stood in no awe of authority. He said, "Why?"

For answer, J.K. tossed him some sort of popular, mimeographed news release from the Washington Office of the Forest Service, an "Uncle Ray's Corner" type of thing, which said that it was impossible to plant longleaf pine because the tap roots were too long to lift the plant without injury and the slightest injury to the tap root would be fatal.

This blurb, (which I never saw myself and the authorship of which I was unable to trace), didn't impress Red much. He grunted, stalked out, dug up the longleaf stock, pruned the roots to 6 inches with his jack-knife and planted the seedlings at the junction of the South Pasture Loop and the road to Milt Miley's house. They survived about 30 percent, started height growth the third year after planting and have since been thinned repeatedly for pulpwood and poles. On the strength of this insubordinate venture of Bateman's, the Company planted some 7,000 acres of longleaf 5 years later and the Civilian Conservation Corps planted more longleaf than anything else on the Southern National Forests during the Depression years.

On Saturday, February 25, 1928, I remarked idly to Red, about eight o'clock in the morning, that it was a pity that the persistent wings of longleaf seed prevented our drill-sowing it in the nursery, the way the Company sowed slash with the

William H. (Col. Bill) Sullivan was born in Canada. He moved to Bogalusa in 1907. Under his supervision, the Great Southern Lumber Company erected the first mill in the world to be constructed of steel. In 1920, he initiated his historic planting program based on Hardtner's pioneering work at Urania (Heyward 1963).

"Brig Young" seeder introduced from Ann Arbor by H.C. Mitchell. By noon Red had perfected the drill seeder and had gone over from broadcast to drill-sowing of longleaf seed. With this seeder, two men easily sowed two hundred 5-foot drills an hour, an economically feasible rate with labor at $1.50 per 10-hour day. Tripping the hinged trough of the seeder with the high handles did away with the stooping and kneeling which had made all previous longleaf seeders impracticable. Aluminum measuring cups, cut down from jello molds in the light of a few seed counts and a shrewdly estimated germination percent, gave entirely adequate control of sowing rate and seedbed density. This effective solution of a practical problem in a matter of hours was characteristic of Red Bateman. So was his acceptance of my unintentional challenge concerning the manageability of his favorite species, longleaf pine.

Even more noteworthy than Red's development of planting techniques was his consistently successful natural reproduction of longleaf from old-growth stands.

At the time of which I am writing, the Forest Service and H.H. Chapman, if they agreed on nothing else, agreed and in print, that longleaf seedlings could not survive in the shade of mature trees. Red, who got his information in the woods instead of from print, knew better. He knew that seedlings did survive, for a few years at least, under the open canopy

Red Bateman's drill for sowing longleaf pine seeds on a nursery bed. This tool greatly improved seedling quality by controlling spacing of the plants.

characteristic of old-growth stands—provided winter fires did not wipe then out in the cotyledon stage.

The Great Southern Lumber Company had a Department of Naval Stores, which chipped all old-growth timber for 2 years before it was cut. In common with all naval stores operators at the time, this Department's practice was to rake a 2-foot clear circle around each tree in the late winter or early spring and then burn over the entire area, to protect the turpentine faces and expensive cups from fires later on. Longleaf

J.K. Johnson, forester for the Great Southern Lumber Company, was one of the first industrial foresters in the country. He was held in high esteem by Wakeley who named the J.K. Johnson Tract of the Palustris Experimental Forest in his honor (Campbell 1976).

seed germinates in November or December. These winter turpentine burns therefore caught the seedlings at their one completely vulnerable stage and effectively prevented natural reproduction.

Red got these facts across to Colonel Sullivan. Sullivan told the man at the head of the Naval Stores Department to go ahead and rake as usual but to quit burning. The man—I forget his name—demurred. "All right," said Sullivan., "your department is barely breaking even, anyway. We'll just abolish it and stop naval stores operations altogether. The seedlings are more important."

The man stopped burning, naturally. As a result, Red caught enough advance reproduction from the good longleaf seed crops of 1924, 1927, 1928, and 1932, and it survived well enough till the overhead stands were logged, to restock 45,000 acres at the rate of 850 or more thrifty young longleaf pines per acre. The process was identical with that paraded as a new discovery on pages 13-14 of the Station's 1963 Annual Report and in U.S. Forest Service Research Paper SO-4, 1963. J.K. Johnson used to write us each year exactly what areas Red was going to reproduce, and so far as I could learn from miles of travel over the Company's lands, Red never failed. It's a pity those letters of Johnson's were "disposed of" according to regulations. They would be priceless historical documents today. I know of no other silvicultural operation in the South more remarkable than this "modified shelterwood" operation of Red Bateman's.

Red died of a heart attack in 1941 at the age of 46. I don't think the brief obituary note that I wrote (*Journal of Forestry* 39: 950) is listed among my publications.

THE "EXTENSIVE SURVEY"

In February 1925, after an intra-Station fanfare of trumpets, we launched another primitive enterprise, the "Extensive Survey." A representative of the Washington Office came down to insure its being started properly. We devoted to it all the rolling stock the Station possessed—the Bogalusa and Urania Model-T Fords purchased the fall before. We even had a special extensive-survey looseleaf notebook form printed— on very good paper too. I had looked forward to the survey, expecting it to be a large-scale estimate of forest conditions and forest resources patterned after Averill, Averill and Stevens' Harvard Forest Bul. 6 of 1923, "A Statistical Forest Survey of Seven Towns in Central Massachusetts", which had greatly impressed me during my graduate year at Cornell or after the Swedish National Forest Survey, of which we were beginning to read glowing accounts. The Extensive Survey proved to be nothing like the Harvard or English surveys and bore no slightest resemblance to the current Southern Forest surveys.

Instead of thoroughly sampling a county, an ownership or any other definable area, two carloads of us (later reduced to one) drove to any place rumored to have definite history or any place with a scattering of old trees left after logging or any area previously or recently burned and "ran strip" toward any distant object on which the compass could be sighted to guide us in a straight line. In some inexplicable revulsion from the scientific accuracy of transit and tape that had distinguished the work on the 200-Acre-Tract at Bogalusa, we used surveyors' chains instead of metal tapes; the click of chain-links against a scrub oak stem was the theme song of 1925.

There was rivalry between the crews in the two cars as to which would pile out, set compass, untangle chain and get running first after the Director and the Washington Office man had agreed, as they easily did, that "here" was a place to get some data. Off we went at a good pace, tallying all trees on a strip 1 or 2 chains wide and at every fifth chain counting seedlings on a 1/100-acre plot. On the backs of the field sheets, we recorded "history" (got from hearsay or deduced from suppression cores, fire scars, age of hardwood sprouts and rotted slash and stumps), groundcover, soil (we had a soil auger along), age of seed trees and a multitude of other things. When conditions were monotonously uniform, we sometimes noted "same as preceding" on the backs of the sheets; as we often rearranged the sheets in a different order before giving them permanent, consecutive numbers; this laborsaving notation caused much confusion later on. We delighted especially in running strip on severely burned areas with lots of white ashes, dead seedlings,

brown tree crowns and pitchy fire scars, all of which we recorded in minute detail as evidence that fire was bad.

In the Great Southern Lumber Company's South Pasture Longleaf Pine Tract of 10,000 acres at Bogalusa, we tallied "seed trees" on some 5 miles of strip and counted longleaf seedlings on nearly 100 "quadrats" (more than 80,000 seedlings to the acre on some of them) because this was an area with a very definite history. To be sure, the history already in our files showed that the area had seeded in from the original old-growth timber at or shortly before logging in 1920 or 1921 and that the spindly residual trees had produced no cones since the date of logging, but we tallied the residual trees and seedlings anyway. The exercise at least had the virtue of making me personally familiar with this famous tract, on which Siggers later did most of his definitive work on brown spot needle disease and of giving us our first quantitative record of the seedling stand. As a means of learning how to achieve natural reproduction of longleaf pine, however, the exercise was worthless.

We saw some interesting things on the Extensive Survey. Near Adamstown, Mississippi, for example, on the south side of the Bogalusa-Poplarville highway, in one of the last remaining stands of big, old-growth longleaf pine in the State, we saw what may have been the very last turpentine "boxes" being cut into the butts of the trees. For a couple of weeks too, near

A cutover longleaf pine stand typical of the stands surveyed during the 1920s. Observations had a focus on the 'harmful' effects of wildfire.

The photo was taken in 1931 several years after the "Extensive Survey" began and the car is a later model, but it represents travel at the time. In this photo of a lunch break are (left to right): G.H. Lentz, J.A. Putnam, J.W. Cruikshank, M.M. Lehrbas, and Henry Bull.

Sylacauga, Alabama, on the Kaul Lumber Company holdings, we ceased running strip on random bearings and by starting from monumented section corners, picked up and followed as well as we could the lines run by Franklin W. Reed in 1903 or thereabouts when he was preparing a management plan (U.S. Department Agriculture Forest Serv. Bul. 68. 1905) for that company. From our tallies of stump holes and old stumps, we reconstructed with rather surprising accuracy the stands Reed had estimated and the intensity of cutting he had recommended and the Kaul Lumber Company had carried out.

The longleaf seedlings Reed had envisioned had not; however, come in probably because the land was all open range and razorback hogs were abundant. Station personnel today see perhaps a tenth as many hogs as there were in 1925 and almost none of the old "piney-woods rooter" breed. The saying was that if you picked up a woods-hawg by the ears and his body balanced his head, he was ripe for slaughter but all you got was a pound of lard and a gallon of turpentine. The hard living, the poor food, the bad roads, the interesting episodes and the fun; however, lived longer in memory than any technical findings of the Extensive Survey. There were exciting moments also.

We lived in rooming houses and small-town hotels and ate many meals in small-town cafes. We got so tired of fat bacon with rind along one edge, greasy fried eggs, grits, ham, beans and baking powder biscuits that some of us lost interest even in *good* bacon and eggs and grits for several years.

Hunting hogs with dogs was considered a necessary way for many to provide food for their families.

I still remember the bedbugs in the Pickering Lumber Company camp at which we stayed one night near Haslam, Texas.

On March 10, 1925, Forbes, Shivery, Harry Wiswell and I crossed the river at Mansfield, Louisiana, with our Ford on a 4-car ferry. The ferry was merely a decked-over scow, coaxed along by a small motorboat. As we left the bank, the boat's motor quit. We drifted around the first bend downstream and around the second. A small colored boy was languidly pumping out the scow with a hand pump about the size of those used to inflate footballs. Shivery, saw Forbes watching the tiny stream of water from the pump and remarked: "I was on a ferry like this once and it sank." "Sank!" exclaimed Forbes, "What do you mean, sank?" "Everything sank," said Shivery, perfectly dead-pan. "The bow went down and the two front cars rolled off and sank; then the stern went down and the two back cars rolled off and sank; then the whole ferry sank." Forbes' face was a study.

Harry Wiswell was a dapper, entertaining fellow. I forget where he had got his professional training, perhaps at the University of Maine. His outlook was amusingly cynical. He could upset his digestion by thinking about it and did so toward the end of every month, to insure getting all the sick leave the regulations then allowed Temporary Field Assistants. He used to say: "Someone's got to marry the rich girl; it might just as well be me." And sure enough, he married an heiress worth, I believe, seven million. When I last saw him, about 1937, he and she were living in New Jersey, with a summer home somewhere farther north and a winter home in Miami.

Not that Harry wasn't a competent field man. He was. He was also an excellent saxophone player and, the summer before the Extensive Survey, had played in a roadhouse band at night while helping Wyman in his Starke, Florida, naval stores studies by day. In those days, we were on actual expense, not per diem, and Harry entered an item in his monthly expense account for cleaning and pressing the tuxedo he wore in the band. If he had called it a "suit," it would have got by, but he was as innocent and naive as he was cynical and specified the kind of suit. The Washington Office held up the whole account and wrote down with justifiable asperity to both Forbes and Wyman to find out what kind of naval stores production studies we were conducting that required the wearing of a tuxedo.

Demmon, destined to succeed Forbes as Director of the Southern Station, Zon as Director of the Lake States Station and Haig as Director of the Southeastern Station and to be President of the Society of American Foresters, joined the Extensive Survey party at Nacogdoches on March 17, 1925, the day after the "million-dollar rain" that broke about a nine months' drought in east Texas. Joined us literally in the woods; though we knew when his train or bus was due to arrive, we went to work at the usual time, after making some provision or other to have him conveyed to the work area. Serious business,

running strip on the Extensive Survey. A couple of hours of tallying were worth more than the convenience and morale of a newly recruited future Director.

Forbes, Demmon, Shivery, Wiswell and I spent the night of March 18 in the ghost sawmill town of Etoile, Texas. Mrs. Honeycut, whose husband combined some sort of caretaking function with farming, served us the best supper we had had in many days and Honeycut found sleeping quarters for us. He contrived beds for four of us from residues of the stock in an abandoned store, but said the fifth man would have to sleep at a farmhouse down the road.

Shivery said he would sleep at the farm if it was all right, otherwise someone else would have to, and went off in the Ford to reconnoiter. He soon came back with an odd smile on his face, got out his shaving kit, shaved and returned to the farm, all without saying a word. He said nothing the next morning, either. He resigned from the Forest Service the following year to become Extension Forester of Tennessee. I still regret that I never sent him a collect telegram on some tenth anniversary of this Extensive Survey episode to ask him *why* he shaved at Etoile, Texas, the night of March 18, 1925. I have let more important inquiries go by default, but no other that would have been such fun.

E.L. Demmon replaced Forbes as Director in 1927 and served in that position until 1944. He was the Director of the Southeastern Forest Experiment Station from 1951 to 1956.

I believe it was on April 3, 1925, in the Neches River bottoms on the way to Kirbyville, Texas, that I first noticed and recorded a loblolly pine: a 5-foot seedling, with 4-needled as well as 3-needled fascicles. In later years I realized that the 4-needled habit in loblolly waist-high to head-high was a sign of optimum conditions for growth, as on the Marigold Mining Company's spoil-bank planting near Birmingham and in plantations under deadened blackjack oak on loessal soil near Oxford, Mississippi. It was not till 1951, however, that I discovered that even 1-0 loblolly nursery stock sometimes produced 4-needled fascicles.

At Diboll we mislaid our surveyor's chain or left it behind somehow. To avoid loss of working time, we borrowed a steel tape from the Southern Pine Lumber Company. It was not till we got to the woods that we noticed the tape was marked in varas instead of feet. Oh well, we thought, we'll run strip in varas and convert to English units later. We took quantities of records in varas and returned the tape to the company with thanks. It was months later, in New Orleans, that we discovered that there were varas and varas, anywhere from 32 to 43 inches in length. We never did find out which vara we had used at Diboll and we never did get those particular data straightened out.

Shivery was a taciturn Pennsylvania Dutchman. He tended to be comic in speech, as in his apocryphal story to Forbes about the scow that sank, or silent as when he shaved at Etoile. At Camden, where we got rooms in a private house for the night of March 30, it took him only a sentence or two to persuade our landlady that he was a Pole by birth. His main contribution to conversation the rest of that day was to remark that the landscape reminded him of Poland.

He could, however, speak at length and with great effect when the occasion demanded. It was near Lufkin, as I recall, that four men and boys in a car containing some women and children also, forced our Ford off the road by singularly inept driving. We were headed north, they south, and they accelerated violently to beat us to a bottleneck caused by two cars, also headed south and doubleparked. We had the right of way; the overcrowded oncoming car would not have had to slow down a bit to let us pass the bottleneck first. Nevertheless, it accelerated.

Shivery was driving our Ford. He went into the ditch to prevent a head-on collision and with consummate skill, avoided any serious damage; kept the car going and forty feet or so farther on, pulled back onto the road again and stopped. The noise was terrific; the ditch bank was full of projecting tree roots, many of which our right-hand fenders snapped off.

As Shivery pulled our Ford to a stop, the four men and boys from the car that had precipitated the accident came running back to us, obviously apprehensive and shouting: "Go on!" "You're all right." "Go on, you ain't hurt a mite." This, of course, was almost next to the interested audience of men in the two cars that were double-parked.

Shivery leaned out of our car, beckoned with his thumb and said, "Come here!"

The four came.

"Who in the God damned hell," Shivery asked in a deliberate drawl, "ever told you you could drive a car?" He went on in that vein for at least 10 minutes, or perhaps 15, slowly, bitingly, incisively to the vast entertainment of the double-parked audience, while the women and children leaned out of the culprit car aghast and their men folk drooped and gulped and drooped some more in silence. At the end, Shivery said: "Now get back in your God damned car and go away."

"Yes sir!" they murmured, turned around and plodded off. Shivery started his engine and drove on without further words.

About this time the seasonal demands of other projects caused some shifts in Extensive Survey personnel and some interruptions in the program. I myself spent a couple of weeks in New Orleans on office routine and at Bogalusa and McNeill on reproduction counts. The Survey crew, consisting of Demmon, Shivery, Flip Reynolds and myself reassembled at Sylacauga, Alabama, to re-run Franklin Reed's old lines on the Kaul Lumber Company holdings.

From Sylacauga, we moved to Bergaw, Pender County, North Carolina by way of Asheville and the then Appalachian Station. My personal diary mentions the superior roads in North Carolina—paved roads—in contrast to the gravel and sand-clay or plain dirt roads in the Lower South. (Regardless of roads, our official maximum speed in the Model T was 32 miles per hour.) We completed Survey field work at New Bern, North Carolina on May 16, 1925 and I went by train from there to Starke, Florida to help Wyman on the naval stores studies and to rejoin Chris, who had been staying with the Wymans all spring.

Those 2 weeks or so in the spring of 1925 were the longest official visits I ever paid to North Carolina and were intensely interesting.

In a swamp near Wilmington, I saw for the first and only time, the famous Venus' fly-trap. This had nothing to do with the Extensive Survey, but I am glad that we had enough general scientific curiosity to take time off and watch the hinged leaves of this remarkable insectivorous plant spring shut on the insects we caught and dropped upon them.

We met the McCoy family, a father and two sons, who spelled their name "McCoy" or "McKoy" as fancy dictated at the moment. They were already carrying on a trade in loblolly pine seed, which they continued for many years afterwards. The shifts in spelling caused us considerable trouble in issuing the list of seed dealers appended to the 1931-1941 southern pine cone crop estimates.

The McKoys lived way out in the woods somewhere. Either they or a neighboring family, I forget which, observed the old country custom of covering their floors with a layer of fine white sand which was swept out and renewed each morning. (My impression is that the custom was linked with tobacco-chewing by the men, but this may be doing some very fine people an injustice.) The family in question had a Negro servant adept in the fast-disappearing art of embellishing the sand with intricate and beautiful arabesques when it was first laid down. I am glad to have seen these designs before the art died out entirely.

Somewhere near Burgaw, one of the party recognized and pointed out the first Sonderegger pine I ever saw and I collected a specimen and submitted it to the Washington Office. It was on this specimen that Sudworth based the northern limit of the rather peculiar range of this hybrid ("North Carolina, Louisiana and Texas") as given in his 1927 Check List and repeated in Elbert Little's 1945 Check List. The hybrid, of course, occurs more or less abundantly in all nine States, from Virginia to Texas, in which the parent species, longleaf, and loblolly, grow intermingled. In the 1955 seed lot No. C-151, collected in Nansemond County, Virginia for the Southwide Pine Seed Source Study, more than 60 percent of the seeds produced Sonderegger seedlings.

It was strawberry season during our stay in Pender County. There were few, if any, rural telephones. New York prices were wired into Burgaw every hour or so. Boys posted along all the roads ran what amounted to relay races to carry the quotations to outlying farms and individual growers stopped picking when prices dropped below levels at which they felt they could profit. Berries too ripe to ship were consumed locally. At our boarding house, we had strawberry shortcake three times a day for five or six successive days.

The fare at Mrs. Stokes' and Mrs. Black's boarding house was superb. It did much to recompense us for the poor food we had had during most of the Survey. It was abundant too and most hospitably served. As soon as one of us had the least room on his plate, Mrs. Black and Mrs. Stokes bore down on him, with serving dishes in both hands, urging, "Have some steak. Have ham. Have potatoes." (Meaning sweet potatoes.) "Have white potatoes. Have greens. What will you have?" It was easy to overeat.

One day Mrs. Stokes passed rice. Demmon refused it courteously. I did also; I was already too full for comfort. Mrs. Stokes said perfectly nicely: "It's easy to tell you gentlemen are from the North. You never eat rice."

Shivery, who never ate rice, who deliberately equated grits with the grit given to chickens to supply their craws and who in Texas had claimed to be a Pole, broke his customary silence to drawl, perfectly dead-pan: "Yes, you can tell they're Yankees all right. They never eat rice and they never eat grits. Now me, I'm from the South. I eat all the rice and all the grits I can get. Please pass me the lightbread."

V.H. Sonderegger replaced Forbes as State Forester of Louisiana in 1921. He was a graduate of the Biltmore Forestry School. Professor H.H. Chapman, who described the natural hybrid between longleaf and loblolly pine, named it Pinus Xsondereggeri *(H.H. Chapm.) in recognition of Sonderegger (Chapman 1922).*

Now a fresh platter of hot biscuits had just been set on the table. To ask for baker's bread when hot biscuits were available was, in Mrs. Stokes' and Mrs. Black's establishment, unthinkable. Mrs. Black gasped audibly. Mrs. Stokes shook her head in bewilderment, set down her bowl of rice and the platter of ham or whatnot that she was passing and retreated to the kitchen, still shaking her head. Flip Reynolds snickered aloud and Demmon and I were hard put to it not to do the same, but George Shivery never cracked a smile.

We had one adventure working out of Burgaw that was a good deal more exciting than our near-wreck in Texas.

Two things set the stage for it. One was the fact that we were driving a Department of Agriculture car with the letters "U.S.D.A." on the license plate. This was during Prohibition and in country districts, it was generally believed that the letters stood for "U.S. Dry Agent." In fact, a few months before, a Bureau of Entomology employee had been shot from ambush and killed right near our experimental tract at McNeill, Mississippi on no other grounds than that he was driving a car with such a plate.

The other was that, about the time we arrived in Pender County, a cigarette salesman had been falsely accused of seducing a farmer's wife and had been castrated by a gang led by the young fellow who had actually made the girl pregnant. The gang had been arrested and were being brought to immediate trial in the next county for mayhem. A news item in a county newspaper had mentioned our arrival for the purpose of the Extensive Survey but had run the item right along with the account of the mayhem, without even paragraphing, in such a way that some people had thought we were part of the gang and some had thought we had been involved in the seduction. People on some lands we were taking data had warned us that there had been arrests against us and to be on our guard.

A couple of days later, when we were en route from Burgaw to another town and returned to our car after running a few chains of transects, we found three men armed with shotguns, rifles and revolvers scattering the contents of our suitcases along the highway ditch.

George Shivery was a little ahead of Demmon, Reynolds and me, with the bunched and tied surveyor's chain in his hand.

He strode up to the three armed men, gripped the chain more firmly and said: "What the hell do you think you're doing?"

One of the men turned a shotgun on him and said: "We'll learn you god-damned dry agents to mind your own business!"

Shivery blew up and started to cuss in earnest. I was sure he'd be shot down where he stood. In fact, I fully expected to be shot myself. George blistered the trio: their manners, morals, intellects, education, looks and ancestry with a digression, as I recall, to pay his own respects to the Volstead Act. Before he had finished, the rest of us had gathered our courage and moved up in support, but he didn't need us. When he was

through, the armed men apologized nicely, cleaned up our belongings and repacked them as well as they could and got into their own car and drove off.

Tom Barron had a similar but milder experience, with no firearms in evidence, when he was gathering loblolly cones alone on a logging operation in Livingston Parish, Louisiana in the fall of 1925 for our original geographic seed source study. Again, everything movable was thrown out of the car by some men who assumed U.S.D.A. meant U.S. Dry Agent. Tom's appearance with a sack of unopened pine cones and a calm statement that he was a forester, not a prohibition agent, won a prompt apology.

The Extensive Survey had been undertaken to get scientific data and to train personnel. Its cost, in time and money was, for that period in the Station's development, very high. What was the followup on the field work and what did the whole enterprise net us?

I think it netted us very little.

We consumed much time during the summer of 1925 "counting" the increment cores we had collected (to date cuttings and fires and to calculate the benefits of release) and "analyzing" (the term is charitable) the quantitative and descriptive notes we had taken. Demmon compiled the results in several typescript reports, not very interesting or convincing, and seldom heard of later. Nothing was published on the Survey as a study. Some of the findings were used in preparing "Timber growing and logging and turpentining practices in the Southern Pine Region" and perhaps biased the conclusions presented in that publication. Certainly the choice and descriptions of areas to survey was biased in many instances.

The "Extensive Survey" documented many stands such as this one. The stands were poorly stocked; many were worked for naval stores, and most had little reproduction due to the damage from free ranging hogs.

As for training personnel, Wiswell and Reynolds were temporary employees and left during or right after the Survey. Hine resigned in the fall of 1925 to become State Forester of Louisiana; Shivery and Hadley resigned in 1926; and even Forbes left in 1927 to organize the Allegheny Station. Of those "trained," only Demmon and I remained and from the fall of 1925 on, I was essentially a specialist in artificial reforestation, a subject on which the Survey did not even touch.

I do not consider that classifying the Extensive Survey as a primitive pastime seriously misrepresents the facts. It was fun while it lasted, but it added little to the sum total of human knowledge beyond the fact that Sonderegger pine occurs in North Carolina.

OTHER EVENTS OF THE PRIMITIVE ERA

I can perhaps sum up the rest of the Primitive Era in less space than I have devoted to the Extensive Survey.

After weighing the possibilities of putting me on a $2.00 per diem instead of actual expense, Forbes decided in the summer of 1925 that the Station budget would not stand my being in perpetual travel status and transferred my official headquarters to Bogalusa. By relieving Hadley of most of the work on forestation studies there during the winter of 1925-26, I was to free him for the fire, grazing and reproduction studies at McNeill and for work in other places. When Hadley resigned in 1926 to become Assistant State Forester of Georgia, I was made Project Leader in charge of Forestation (now Regeneration), an assignment from which, incidentally, I was never formally relieved. L.J. Pessin, the first Ph.D. ever employed by the Station, took over the McNeill studies when Hadley left.

It must have been in January 1926 that I requisitioned some paper clips for the Bogalusa Office. Vera Spuhler sent me 12 in an envelope, with a note urging me to use them carefully, as they were all she could allot to the Bogalusa Work Center. The whole Station had one box of gem clips to last the entire Fiscal Year.

What the Forestation Project lacked in paper clips in Fiscal Year 1926, it made up for in Field Assistants.

N.T. ("Tom") Barron, whose later services with the South Carolina Forestry Commission and the Camp Manufacturing Company are well known, was assigned to assist me in the fall of 1925 and helped collect and extract the seed for the Station's original study of geographic sources of loblolly pine. Late in 1925, however, the Great Southern Lumber Company's professional forester, H.C. Mitchell, resigned to become Mississippi's first Extension Forester and Tom left the Station to take Mitchell's place with the Great Southern.

Roy A. Chapman arrived at Bogalusa on January 1, 1926 in the cruising jacket and work pants he had worn on McArdle's Douglas-fir volume- and yield-table crew in the Pacific

Northwest to take Tom's place with me. Roy still had his senior year in forestry at Minnesota to complete but his strong statistical bent was already apparent and he seemed to me, even in 1926, to have more research ability than most of our permanent staff. His later services at this Station and in the Washington Office amply confirmed this impression.

Although we added a second general clerk (Mrs. Nolan) and a computing clerk (Mary Regan, who later became Mrs. Ronald Craig) in the New Orleans Office and later added more to the clerical staff, the professional staff were still spread thinly over our immense territory and we still traded work.

R.A. Chapman did much to lead the Station, and Forest Service research, into the statistical age. He trained with R.A. Fisher for several years and this strengthened his statistical capability.

Initiation of Research on Florida Sand Hills

The present Southern Region of the Forest Service had not yet been set up. The staff of Region 7, in which the Florida and Arkansas National Forests lay, were greatly concerned over the lack of longleaf pine reproduction on the deep sands of the Choctawhatchee National Forest and in 1926 arranged to finance a man to work there, under Station direction. (As we learned by bitter experience, this is not necessarily a sound arrangement.) He was to work on problems of natural reproduction and of artificial reforestation, including introduction of exotics. None of the eucalypts planted by Bristow Adams under Eldredge's supervision 17 or 18 years before had survived, only three maritime pines were left on the thousand or so acres seeded and planted to this species by Eldredge in 1910 and 1911, and it was felt that some other exotic species should be tried. The native sand pine seems not to have been considered, perhaps because it could hardly be called a "timber" tree and the present pulpwood market for it was not yet dreamed of.

To get the Choctawhatchee Project going well, there was, first and last, a tremendous gathering at Camp Pinchot on the Choctawhatchee Forest—Assistant Chiefs E.E. ("Nick") Carter (Timber Management) and Earl Clapp (Research), Assistant Regional Forester Robie Evans of Region 7, B.H. Paul and Dr. Eloise Gerry of the Forest Products Laboratory, Supervisor Hill and Ranger McKee of the Forest, Len Wyman of the Station staff at Starke, Florida (who brought Mrs. Wyman and little Ruth with him), Forbes and myself from the New Orleans Office (I had moved from Bogalusa to New Orleans by this time) and the new man assigned to the Project, Edgar A. ("Al") Smith. Forbes had had Wyman bring over the Starke Ford for the party's use because Starke and Camp Pinchot were both in the same State and was embarrassed when Wyman pointed out that Starke was twice as far away from Camp Pinchot as New Orleans was.

Al Smith was a most interesting man. He had topped off his professional training at Mont Alto by taking one of Schenck's European tours. Alone of all forestry students I have ever known, he systematically bought a book on the same subject but by a different author to match each text required in his professional courses and had acquired insight and perspective beyond his years after thoughtful comparison of the two books in each pair. He had a keen mind and an avid curiosity and was a glutton for work. He prepared well for the new undertaking.

We lost Al on October 23, 1926, before all the party convening to start him on his job had arrived. The day was warm and he had gone swimming by himself in Garnier's Bayou after work; I remember his leotard-type green bathing suit vividly. Little Ruth Wyman was sailing a toy boat and an off-shore breeze carried it out, near center, to where the water was about 10 feet deep. Al swam over to retrieve the boat, got his hand on it, capsized it and sank without a sound or any appreciable struggle. Wyman and I realized he was in trouble and went in after him, fully dressed. I got Al's body to the surface, but impeded as I was by heavy clothing and high boots, lost it. An Assistant Ranger named Anchors had vaulted a nearby fence carrying a heavy plank on his shoulder (he was unable to vault the same fence afterwards even without the plank!) and got the plank out to me at considerable risk to himself, as he could not swim. I maneuvered the plank to a position over Al, got him up a second time, and with the help of several in a boat, got him ashore.

Hill lost his job as Supervisor as an aftermath of the affair. There had been a severe storm some weeks before, but he had not got the Forest phone lines or roads repaired, though the fire season was imminent and Nick Carter and Robie Evans were there to see the results. We couldn't phone for a doctor. Mrs. Wyman had to drive us to Niceville to get one and the road was so badly washed out that she broke a car spring.

We applied artificial respiration until the doctor arrived an hour or more later but without much hope. There seemed to be no water in Al's lungs. When the doctor finally came, he told us that Al had been dead before he slipped under the surface. Under Florida law, the death was classified as "accidental, while in the water," or in some such phrase; this made good the double-indemnity term of his insurance policy. The actual cause of death, however, was heart failure, unusual in one so young.

Al's estate never did receive the pay for his brief service with the federal government because, in addition to neglecting the roads and phone lines, Supervisor Hill had neglected to sign and forward the oath of office that Al had executed. The Service was powerless to disburse the money and had to content itself with reducing Hill from Supervisor to Road Foreman.

Al's tragic death and the sloppy administrative procedure it revealed were depressing. The postponement of the Camp Pinchot Project till Gemmer was assigned to it about a year later was depressing too. So also was a little work with B.H. Paul of the Laboratory, just after Al died.

Paul was there to collect specimens of longleaf pine from moist to excessively dry sites for a study of influences affecting wood specific gravity. Paul bossed the job; Wyman and I pulled the saw. As I recall, Paul accepted the first five trees we cut on the dry site as none of them had a very large percentage of summerwood. On the moist site, however, he kept us cutting trees and cutting trees until we had found five with high percentages of dense summerwood. (Even as an undergraduate, Roy Chapman would not have condoned working in this manner.) I have been skeptical of B.H. Paul's investigations on specific gravity ever since.

Recruits and Visitors

As the Primitive Era progressed, our staff changed considerably as we gradually grew. New professional employees replaced those who resigned and left, in turn, some even to return again. L.I. Barrett was here at this time. So were L.J. ("Doc") Pessin, W.G. Wahlenberg, William Lentz, each for the first of two appointments. Marie Turnbull and Mrs. Black joined the clerical staff.

Nowadays, we count our visitors to Crossett, the Institute of Genetics and other Centers in hundreds and even in thousands every year. Though fewer, there were visitors during the Primitive Era who were interesting and on occasion famous. Numbers of them wanted to see things throughout our territory, but Bogalusa was the greatest operation, greater even than Henry Hardtner's operation at Urania.

By the spring of 1926, the Great Southern Lumber Company had established 12,700 acres of successful southern pine plantations at Bogalusa. No other single agency south of Biltmore, North Carolina had a hundred acres. The Bogalusa plantations drew visitors not only from all over the United States but from all over the world. My recollection is that, first and last, I have personally shown the sights at Bogalusa to more than 24 State Foresters and to foresters and other

Wakeley, with George Turner of Darington Hall, Ltd., Totnes, S. Deron, UK, in 1931, at a Great Southern Lumber Company natural longleaf pine stand resulting from the 1920 seed crop.

professional people from at least 20 and probably 30 foreign countries.

The Association of State Foresters met at Bogalusa December 2, 1924, as guests of the Great Southern Lumber Company for 3 days. (The Company charged their hotel expenses to that year's planting costs.) The great Tor Jonson visited Bogalusa in September 1925; despite the language barrier, he and the Company's Head Ranger, F.O. ("Red") Bateman, discussed the silviculture of the future in terms that staggered the imagination of the Station staff, but that the decades showed to have been prophetic. Other Swedish visitors included Ehrenborg, who had worked on the first Swedish Forest Survey ("Our boys rhan mahdly through the woods, sthecreaming 'Tventy mehters! Thirty mehters! Forty mehters! at the tops of their voices"), Eric Ostlin (who held a brief temporary job on our own staff), a paper chemist named Nilsson (who had a 1-year Scandinavian-American Industrial Fellowship with the Great Southern) and in 1927 Hendrik Hesselnan, who visited Bogalusa with Dr. Carl Hartley and Dr. Reginald Colley of the Bureau of Plant Industry.

Hesselman's English was poor—he had, in fact, an interpreter with him—but he spoke both German and Esperanto fluently, as did Colley. Hartley spoke German fluently, but not Esperanto. Hesselman, I think, never realized Colley's trick of shifting the conversation to Esperanto to tease Hartley or the suavity with which Hartley shifted it back to German again.

Another interesting visitor, in 1925, was a Mr. Bens, who had invented, and was trying out on the Company's old-growth longleaf pine, the prototype of the modern power saw.

Lost Opportunities

We missed some tricks during the Primitive Era, the most notable of which, perhaps, had to do with the dormancy of pine seed, particularly loblolly. N.D. Canterbury, who was Assistant State Forester in Charge of Management under State Forester Hine of Louisiana, appealed to us for help on this problem and got nowhere. In the fall of 1927, therefore, he sent seed of the four principal species to Dr. Lela V. Barton at Boyce Thompson Institute for Plant Research. In a few months, she developed the process of moist, cold stratification essentially as it is still used today and published as results in *Journal of Forestry* 26: 774-785, 1928. She used the surplus seed from that shipment and from a similar shipment that Canterbury sent her the following year for a comprehensive storage study. The results of this storage study, which she published in 1935, first demonstrated the feasibility of storing southern pine seed below 32 °F.

Following the leads of Louisiana and Texas, a number of other states established State forest nurseries from 1926 on. Practically all grew at least two species of southern pine and several grew three or four. I believe that, if I had had the forethought to propose it, the State Foresters would have agreed to give away a complimentary sample of 100 seedlings of a different species with each order of 5,000 trees or more. If this had been done and each gift sample had been

Nathan Canterbury was a well trained graduate from Yale University. His tenure as Louisiana State Forester was limited to one month and one day due to a political patronage situation.

Forest tree nurseries were installed in many locations in the late 1920s. This is the Longbell Lumber Company nursery at DeRidder, LA in 1928.

marked with a tag requesting the recipient to plant the gift trees in a staked row in the middle of his plantation, we would by 1930, have laid the foundation for a Southwide study to offer choice of species for site. I reproach myself for having overlooked this golden opportunity. Choice of species for site is, in numerous localities throughout the South, an important problem still awaiting adequate attack.

PROGRESS AND GROWING PAINS

Despite the paucity of our resources and the shortcomings of our research techniques, we laid some sound foundations during the Primitive Era. The volume, stand and yield tables in Miscellaneous Publication 50 were a substantial achievement in themselves. Although long since largely outmoded, they accomplished their purpose.

Wyman's work on gum naval stores production revolutionized the naval stores industry in some ways as drastically as the introduction of the cup and gutter had done a quarter of a century before. It laid the foundations, furthermore, for the subsequent development of bark chipping with acid treatment and for present day research on the genetical control of oleoresin production.

Coordination of the Station's artificial reforestation studies with the Great Southern Lumber Company's planting program, through our transfer of our work from McNeill to Bogalusa, certainly expedited research in this field. Had the move not been made Technical Bulletin 492 almost certainly would not have been published in time to serve as a planting handbook for the Civilian Conservation Corps in the Southern Pine Region.

In view of the use that was made of Bulletin 492 during the CCC period and of its sequel, Agriculture Monograph 18, during the post World-War II planting boom, perhaps my own fortuitous routing to Bogalusa in 1924 and my formal assignment as Regeneration Project Leader in 1926 may also be counted as constructive.

My immensely detailed records of individual trees in the experimental plantations at Bogalusa are proving to be a treasure-trove of information. The existence of those records was one of the considerations that resulted in establishing the Institute of Forest Genetics at Gulfport. Not least important was the fact that under the stimulus of an October 1925 visit from Lloyd Austin, the first Director of the then Eddy Tree Breeding Station at Placerville, I began to designate potential plus trees in the plantations as early as 1928.

The establishment of our original loblolly seed-source study at Bogalusa, under the personal urging of Chief Forester Greeley, proved to be epoch-making.

Our initial employment of Roy Chapman as a Temporary Field Assistant in 1926 and his subsequent permanent appointment in 1929 resulted in the salvation of the Station's statistical reputation. Undoubtedly, if Roy had not been here, other persons or events would ultimately have coerced us into ways of statistical rectitude. Roy's timely arrival made the Southern Station a leader in this field.

In contradistinction to the sophisticated, large scale and sometimes rather mechanical approach that has resulted from the statistical techniques inculcated by Roy Chapman and others, some of us laid great stress in the early days on search, observation and description. We turned over litter, dissected cones and trigs, reported what we saw and sent specimens to specialists for identification. Today, we are too busy measuring

Wyman's research in naval stores changed the hack size to a smaller one that was more efficient and less labor intensive.

"Scoring" Research

One was a tendency to express the current progress and total accomplishment of individual Stations and of the Branch of Research in quantitative terms. We began to receive lists of the numbers of permanent sample plots established by the various Stations. As I remember, there were heated arguments as to how large a plot had to be to qualify; must it be at least a fifth of an acre or did a 1/100-acre "quadrat" count as a permanent sample plot? Regardless of how a decision on this point affected the apparent relative standing of rival Stations, the figures really meant very little, as the treatments applied to the plots were seldom if ever replicated and some were applied without controls or checks or indeed without any definable purpose.

I question, though, whether today's vaunted lists of articles published each year or the Washington Office's score sheet of titles published per thousand dollars of appropriations, mean any more than the old lists of permanent plots established. Under today's system, a title is a title; my 3-sentence contribution to *Southern Forestry Notes* 79, of May 1952, counted no more, no less, than my 233-page *Agriculture Monograph* representing a quartercentury of intensive research. Furthermore, articles authored jointly by men in two different Stations are becoming commonplace, and any such article is listed by both Stations.

our quotas of randomized, replicated plots to do these things. I yield to no man in my admiration of statistical sensitivity and rigor, but I still recognize research potentialities of the man—a W.W. Ashe, a Paul Siggers, or a L.M. Ware—with a trained mind, a lively curiosity and a plain curiosity. My early descriptive notes on trees planted at Bogalusa are valuable source material for Bulletin 492 and Agriculture Monograph 18 and are yielding a new round of dividends as we plan genetics research. A case in point is the mass of longleaf and oak roots Gene Gemmer and I excavated and photographed at Camp Pinchot in 1927. It was not until 1958 that a better photograph was taken to illustrate Occasional Paper 161. For why? Because in the intervening 31 years, nobody had had the time or perseverance to make a similar excavation!

I feel that even my 1926 trip with Ashe to scout out the future Kisatchie National Forest was foundation laying of a sort. The Kisatchie had been the field laboratory of the Alexandria Research Center. The Alexandria Research Center has made substantial contributions—in poisoning undesirable hardwoods and in direct seeding, to mention only two.

By the end of the Primitive Era, there were portents of two phenomena that were to loom larger in later years.

Wakeley's "Planting the Southern Pines" became the source of information used to reforest the southern pine region (Wakeley 1954). Although long out of print, it is still frequently cited and was one of the most significant early documents from the Southern Station.

"Command-Performance" Publications

Our other forewarning, had we but realized it, was of what may be called the "command-performance" publication.

Such a publication may be a single unit of regional or national scope or may be a regional or local item in a Service-wide series. Characteristically, it is conceived not by the authors but by someone having line authority over them. I say "authors" advisedly; there are usually at least two, and often many, and their names may appear in the published work only in a footnote credit-line, if at all. As a rule, the publication is demanded before the research on which it is allegedly based has been completed and in extreme cases before the research has been started; the published conclusions are, therefore, to be premature. My jaundiced personal impression is that the deadline for completion of the manuscript usually coincides with seasonally exacting field work of particularly high priority, such as cone collection, experimental prescribed burning or the planting of irreplaceable nursery stock.

Over the years, the Southern Station has had a hand in many such publications. Examples are the "Flood Study" (*Relation of forestry to the control of floods in the Mississippi Valley*, 70th Cong. 2nd Sess. House Doc. 573. (740 pp., illus. 1929), the Copeland Report, the Woody Plant Seed Manual, the

Lewis Grosenbaugh continued the statistical excellence in the Southern Station started by Roy Chapman. He was given the U.S. Department of Agriculture Superior Service Award in 1959 for his contributions in mensuration technology that revolutionized stand measurements.

Timber Resources Review ("T.R.R.") and several Yearbook of Agriculture articles. On the local level, our modern Annual Reports have every undesirable characteristic of command performance publications except one. They are imposed by the authority and divert a great number of authors from original research for a total of many precious weeks each year. Only Lew Grosenbaugh's recent limitation of their contents, mainly to summaries of research already published elsewhere, has reduced to tolerable levels their content of premature conclusions.

The first command-performance publication of which we were acutely conscious was the "Flood Study" which cast a pall over the summers of 1927 and 1928. The Station's very first encounter with the genus, however, was with the series originally spoken of as the "Minimum Requirements and Desirable Practice" bulletins—more familiarly as the "Minnie Reck" bulletins. In print, the series appeared as "Timber Growing and Logging Practice" bulletins. One must assume that the wording was changed to avoid the implication of government regulation of cutting on private land, which was then a highly controversial subject and which the word *requirements* would automatically have called to mind.

The idea of the Minnie Reck series must have antedated the establishment of the Southern Station. Certainly it strongly colored the Station's original investigative programs; witness the installation of the "minimum requirements" and "desirable practice" blocks in the 200-Acre Tract at Bogalusa. The main emphasis of the Extensive Surveys of 1925 and 1926 was upon gathering material for the Station's contribution to the series and I do not think that it distorts the truth to say that the bulletin's conclusions—the efficacy of scattered seed trees and the evils of any burning whatsoever—had already been formulated and that survey areas were deliberately selected to support them.

The earliest explicit statement concerning the Southern Station's contribution to the series seems to be Forbes' written proposal of August 15, 1925, that it be a 32-page bulletin with 16 illustrations. My impression is that he intended to submit the manuscript within the next 12 months.

Forbes' "Timber growing and logging and turpentining practices of the Southern Pine Region" actually appeared as U.S. Dept. Agr. Tech. Bul. 204 in 1930, 3 years after he had left the Southern for the Forest Service Allegheny Station. Its length, 115 pages! Despite the care lavished upon it by the staff and especially by Forbes himself, it seemed to me when it appeared, and still seems to me, one of the greater contributions to the series. As with the characters and events in paper-back mystery stories, any resemblance of the practices recommended in Tech. Bul. 204 to those that are the backbone of Southern pine forestry today is "purely coincidental." The Bulletin stands as a monument and a largely forgotten monument at that, both to the command-performance publication and to the Primitive Era at the Southern Station.

THE SOUTH PASTURE FIRE OF 1928

The morning of March 21, 1928 at Bogalusa was clear with a strong, gusty north wind. I was in the midst of the third-year re-examination of the experimental plantations at Coburn's Creek and had an 8 o'clock appointment with J.K. Johnson, head of the Great Southern Lumber Company's Forestry Department, and his staff, to discuss the work on the ground.

Red Bateman, the Company's Head Ranger, and his younger brother, Bryant, arrived before J.K., while the young slash pines I was measuring, were still sparkling with dew. Bryant was a recent graduate of the L.S.U. School of Forestry and was junior to Paul Garrison under J.K. He had been my field assistant for a short time while still a student, and as a matter of course, relieved me of the tally board and took notes for me while we waited for J.K. We went down one 33-foot row and back up the next in the familiar routine. Red ambled along beside us, making jokes.

At the uphill end of the second row, Red looked off across the plantation and said: "You know, young slash pine always puts me in mind of a little boy going along with his face washed, all proud."

My own firstborn, a son, was two and a half at the time and I knew exactly what Red meant. Furthermore, no dendrology text or technical bulletin has ever rendered so precisely the essence of a pure stand of young slash pine before it has been hit by fusiform rust. Red's description is sheer poetry. I included it in the text of Technical Bulletin 492 and again in the text of Agriculture Monograph 18, but higher authority deleted it from the former as too undignified for Departmental publication, and from the latter to save space.

We were just starting to remeasure the third row of trees when J.K. Johnson drove up, and we stopped routine work for a general tour of the experimental plantations and some Company plantations nearby.

During our tour of the Company plantations, a great smoke boiled up to the northwest of us, obviously from Company land. By then, the wind was very strong. J.K. and the Batemans left in hot haste for the fire and I resumed remeasurements at Coburn's Creek.

The fire was in the South Pasture Longleaf Pine Tract, ten thousand acres densely stocked with seedlings from the bumper 1920 seed crop on old-growth timber. Red Bateman, realizing the silvicultural possibilities of the phenomenal seedling catch, had persuaded Colonel Sullivan, the Company

Fire control was done with the use of "fire flaps" before the development of fire plows and the knowledge of backfiring technology.

Manager, to fence the area against hogs and had cut it up into quarter sections with a series of 100-foot-wide, annually burned firebreaks. In the spring of 1928, all but a tiny percentage of the longleaf seedlings were still hidden in the 7 years' accumulation of unburned grass and were terrifically infected with brown spot.

Four rural residents, who presumably liked big fires better than big corporations, chose dry, windy March 21, just as the seedlings were putting out new needles, to cut the phone line between the lookout tower and town, drive in on the South Pasture Loop, walk some distance in to a north-south firebreak and set fires on both sides of it and just south of an east-west break. They left these two fires to run wild over a quarter of a square mile apiece, returned to their car and drove half a mile north to repeat the process.

They failed; however, to reckon with the Company-State detection system.

The country was open and the lookout saw the first two fires almost instantly, before their separate smokes merged. When he tried to phone company headquarters and found the line dead, he suspected what was up; a few minutes later, when he saw the dust raised by the incendiaries' car as they drove north on the Loop, he was sure of it. Meanwhile, he had called on a second uncut line to a logging camp north of the fire and the camp had relayed the call to town. From camp and town, more than 50 men started at once for the fire and Red Bateman, who drove like Jehu, was already on the way from a house closer by. The result was that the culprits were caught in the act, moments after setting their second pair of fires.

Despite the promptness of detection and the speed and vigor of attack, the fire covered 800 acres. It was very hot and very fast. This was 17 years or more before Art Shepard pioneered the "Ranger's Pal" fire plow and only bold, skillful backfiring

from pre-burned breaks stopped the head and the foreward flanks. Breaks stopped the main flanks. Only the rear was whipped out with "fire flaps"—hoe handles with 30-inch lengths of machine belting riveted on the ends.

We at the Southern Station regretted that an ideal cooperator the Great Southern Lumber Company should suffer such a fire. Nevertheless, we rejoiced in the opportunity it gave us.

Fire and Brown Spot

At the time of the fire, we were in controversy with H.H. Chapman concerning the interrelationships of brown spot and fire. In his Yale Forest School Bulletin 16, published in 1926, he had stated categorically that fire would control brown spot. We had learned enough about brown spot by 1928 to feel sure that it would rather promptly invade even very extensive burns. Here, in the midst of 10,000 acres densely stocked with heavily infected longleaf seedlings, was more than a square mile essentially freed of inoculum by a single fire, and a fire, moreover, larger and a good deal hotter than Chapman advocated. By March 31, the tenth day after the fire, I had finished laying out a row of 100-seedling permanent plots from the margin of the burn to its center, with a check plot outside the burn. We would find out who was right, we or Chapman.

Laying out those plots was a fascinating job. I had excellent help, a Temporary Field Assistant named Gil Hills and a brilliant, local high-school student named Spurgeon Wingo, the son of a Baptist minister. They were extraordinarily inquisitive individuals. Hills, for example, had dropped lady beetles from a fourth-floor window in Boston and rushed downstairs to see if they were hurt by the fall and at Bogalusa had squeezed his luncheon orange into a small pond to see how pollywogs reacted to a change in pH. Spurgeon Wingo

The development of equipment such as the "Ranger's Pal" fire plow did much to make control of wildfire easier and more successful.

H.H. Chapman measuring the effect of fire on longleaf pine seedling growth. The controversy on effects of fire between Chapman and Forest Service specialists continued for a number of years. Gradually, the Forest Service began to accept the beneficial efforts of fire on the management of longleaf pine.

was full of similar tricks. All three of us found much on the burn to excite curiosity.

There were quantities of dead, headless beetles among the ashes and we came across several large, dead snakes whose bellies had been blown open by the steam generated inside them as the fire swept over them. The inner bark of scrub oaks 3 and 4 inches in diameter had been killed and was fermenting. The 7-year-old longleaf seedlings—they averaged 20 to 50 thousand to the acre—had been reduced to blackened nubs, but only the minute fraction of them that had started height growth had been killed. Ten days after the fire, the needles of the innumerable smaller seedlings had resumed growth and showed new green tissue below charred stubs left by the fire. We, at the Station, were right about the promptness with which brown spot would reinvade big burned areas. My personal diary for June 25, 1928, records unmistakable infection on the new foliage all over the 800-acre burn in South Pasture. By the following September, the longleaf seedlings within the burn seemed as heavily infected as they had ever been. But—and this taught us a wholesome lesson— the seedlings within the burn started height growth 3 years before the seedlings outside the burn. By the time this fact was evident, we had become mature enough in outlook so that our satisfaction with the information gained outweighed our

annoyance that Chapman had also been right in his contention regarding fire. Today, the 800-acre burn is one of the most beautiful longleaf pine stands in the South. Between 1945 or thereabouts and 1960, it was thinned two or three times for pulpwood and in 1964, another thinning yielded a lucrative cut of poles.

There is a certain irony associated with this superior growth of the longleaf within the burn. My personal diary of April 6, 1928, records that two of the men who set the fire on March 21 had already been tried and had been fined fifty dollars apiece and that the other two had been fined $200 apiece and given 90 days in jail. My recollection is that it was on this occasion that one or more of the men had pleaded ignorance as a defense, only to be reminded sharply by the judge of previous sentences for woods-burning imposed by the same court. I learned afterwards, that lacking cash to pay, the two men fined $200 each had had to work out their fines on the Parish roads at 10¢ an hour. This took them into the following year, whereby they lost the year's crops and the mortgages on their farms were foreclosed. They moved to Mississippi, and with their going, incendiarism on the Company holdings around Bogalusa practically ceased until 1934 or 1935, when jealous young bloods began setting fires on Saturday nights to break up the dances in the local CCC camp.

Wakeley's and his colleagues' studies on the effects of fire did much to change the Forest Service's thinking that all fire was harmful.

Ironical or not, the sentences were just enough. Even though this particular fire did more good than harm, the decision to burn would rest with the owner and manager, not with his spiteful neighbors.

The study of the rate of brown-spot invasion was only the beginning of the benefits we reaped from the March 21 fire.

Brown Spot and Fungicides

I wrote a memorandum of establishment describing the string of plots I had run into the center of the burn and the isolated unburned check plot outside. As a matter of professional courtesy and common interest, we sent a copy of the memorandum to Dr. Carl Hartley, Forest Pathologist in the old Bureau of Plant Industry in Washington. Carl was one of our most cordial and stimulating cooperators, and a brilliant young products pathologist, Ralph Lindgren, had already started work at the Station, on sap stain control, under his direction.

Carl replied by wire on April 16, saying he hoped to get a tree disease pathologist assigned to the Station early in the fiscal year beginning July 1, and urging us to put in additional plots on the unburned area and to control brown spot on them with fungicides, to further elucidate the separate and combined effects of brown spot and fire on longleaf seedlings in the grass stage. He sent us a supply of ready-mixed Bordeaux powder (for which the then more effective home-mixed was later substituted), and wrote several times suggesting details, including the spraying of some plots with lime-sulfur instead of Bordeaux lest the copper in the Bordeaux complicate results by stimulating growth.

On April 24, 1928, I laid out two series of square-milacre plots in a very dense longleaf seedling stand near the burn, to be sprayed with Bordeaux, and on April 25 a series to be sprayed with lime-sulfur. Of the two Bordeaux series, one was to be sprayed at 2-week intervals throughout the growing season. In the other, one plot was to be sprayed at once, it and a second plot 2 weeks later; these two and a third at the end of 4 weeks, and so on, to determine infection dates. Unsprayed check milacres were sandwiched in between the sprayed milacres of both series. The Great Southern Lumber Company undertook to do the spraying and Bryant Bateman did it conscientiously and well, with a burlap screen draped around each plot to keep the fungicide from drifting to the unsprayed checks. Hartley was unable to get the promised pathologist till late in the calendar year and much of the credit for the success of the experiment that past season is rightfully Bry Bateman's.

The experiment succeeded beyond our wildest hopes. Within 3 or 4 years, it gave us a wealth of data on the effects of brown spot on survival and growth. Even in the first few weeks, it gave us valuable information on the life history of the brown-spot pathogen and on the effectiveness of fungicides.

It had immediate and far-reaching practical results as well. The Great Southern's 1928 nursery was mostly in longleaf seedlings—some 7 million of them—the quality of which could be greatly reduced by brown-spot infection. There was plenty of inoculum all around the nursery. By the time this nursery stock had begun to develop second-year foliage, the

Nursery workers at the Stuart Nursery in central Louisiana spraying longleaf pine seedlings with the Bordeaux mixture that effectively controlled brown-spot needle disease of longleaf pine seedlings.

Bryant Bateman, brother of Great Southern's Head Ranger Red Bateman, became the first forestry graduate of LSU. Later, he served on the LSU faculty for many years.

1928 foliage on our unsprayed checks in South Pasture was heavily infected, but the new needles on the seedlings in the plots sprayed biweekly were practically without a lesion. The Great Southern foresters were quick to make use of the findings. They sprayed the longleaf nursery stock at intervals throughout the summer and took it to the field in excellent condition the following winter. Fungicidal control of brown spot on longleaf seedlings has been standard practice in southern pine nurseries ever since.

Before I accepted Carl Hartley's offer of fungicides and a sprayer and installed the plots, I got permission from Director Demmon to start the study, but I did not discuss details with him. And inspired by some delvings in statistical texts, I replicated treatments. In the lime-sulfur series, I installed 2 treatments (sprayed and check) x 4 replications. In the biweekly Bordeaux series, I installed 2 treatments (sprayed and check) x 10 replications or 20 observations in all, on square milacre plots. The extravagance of the latter layout incurred some criticism from Demmon and more from the Washington Office later on. To the best of my knowledge, however, these sprayed and unsprayed plots in the South Pasture Longleaf Pine Tract were the first replications ever installed by the Southern Station for the express purpose of providing an estimate of error.

One other consequence of the big 1928 fire deserves introductory mention here. Hartley finally recruited and assigned to us the promised forest pathologist. The pathologist was Paul V. Siggers, one of the hardest and most productive workers the Station ever had, one of its best writers and critics of writing, and one of the most lovable characters its staff has ever known.

THE ERA OF EXPANSION AND RECOGNITION

I always think of the Era of Expansion and Recognition as having begun with the South Pasture fire of 1928. True, the expansion grew out of legislation and appropriations in no wise connected with the fire. The recognition was won by studies unrelated to the fire. Nevertheless, the studies and projects stemming from the fire, and many others that were started at the same time or shortly afterwards, outranked in object and in execution almost all of the studies of the Primitive Era. As a group, they constituted a turning-point in the Station's history.

Improved Approach and Execution

Perhaps one of my own studies, started in the First Era but completed in the Second, will illustrate what I mean.

By 1927 I had become interested enough in damage to loblolly and shortleaf pine by the Nantucket tip moth, (*Rhyacionia frustrana* Comstock), to want to do something about it! The logical point of attack seemed to be to learn the life history of the insect, which appeared to be related in some way to the multinodal habit of the preferred hosts. I admit that I was spurred on to the study by the opinion of a visiting Swedish entomologist, Dr. Ivar Trägordh, that the life cycle must be

Tip moth is a common problem in loblolly pine plantations and a number of insecticides have been developed to control the insect and limit the amount of damage. More recent studies indicate that the seedlings generally recover from the damage later in the sapling stage.

2 years. His opinion struck me as absurd. Tip moths occurred in 10-months-old loblolly seedlings in the Great Southern Lumber Company's City Hall nursery at Bogalusa, and I couldn't visualize the larvae from a previous year's brood making their way by thousands across a broad gravel street to burrow into seedlings of the current year. Even without Dr. Trägordh's odd assumption, however, the damage done to our experimental plantations by the tip moth was challenge enough.

I had been taking notes for at least a year or two on larval and nymphal stages and on flights of adults when, in the fall of 1927, I started bagging infested loblolly tops with voile and noting dates of larval emergence and of new infestations inside the bags. As nearly as I can tell from my official diary, I put the first bags in place October 11, 1927.

During the long period of spring plantation re-examination at Bogalusa in 1928, and as other Bogalusa trips offered opportunity during the late spring and early summer of that year, I kept close track of moths in these cages and among uncaged trees nearby and considerably sharpened my impressions of the life cycle.

Then the unexpected happened. The Washington Office wrote, early in July urging us to contribute a paper on some forest insect—any insect—to the Fourth International Congress of Entomology to be held at Cornell in mid-August. All we had to offer —we had no entomologist on the staff—was my tip moth notes, which I wrote up and, on July 24, submitted to Washington.

To my utter surprise, Washington not only accepted the paper, which of course was based on observations only, not experiments, but authorized my attending the Congress to present it. This was quite all right with me as it meant a free trip back to my university, a few days with my father- and mother-in-law in Ithaca, and, at the cost of a little annual leave en route, a visit to relatives in Rochester. Station finances, to be sure, were so straitened that I had to travel at summer tourist rates and go to Niagara Falls on the way home to get my tourist ticket validated, but that was all right too. I paid my own way across the International Bridge while there to see the falls for 30 minutes from the Canadian side; to date, this has been my only visit to a foreign country.

After I had registered for the Congress, I discovered that the Washington office had taken no steps to get my paper on the program, which was by invitation only. By pulling wires with Professor Merrick, under whom I had taken entomology and who was on some Congress committee, I got permission to "propose" the paper to the section on Forest Entomology. I read the paper by viva voce, permission of the entomologists in that section, who generously postponed luncheon for 10 minutes to hear it. It came immediately after a quarterly summary of his doctoral dissertation on white pine weevil, also a shoot-boring insect, by one Barnes, and seemed terribly trivial and shoddy by comparison. I felt greatly subdued.

I felt worse when I got back to New Orleans and both Director Demmon and I received letters of reprimand from the Washington Office for having submitted the paper in the first place. It seems that Dr. F.C. Craighead had taken offense at a mere forester's having assumed to publish concerning an insect and had taken steps to prevent my repeating the outrage. Nevertheless, the deed was done. My paper was printed in the Proceedings of the Fourth Congress (Volume II, pages 865-868, 1929).

It astonishes me today that I wrote that paper as soundly as I did on such slender evidence. Immediately following the Congress, I felt that my tentative conclusions were open to serious question. In the new spirit of the Second Era, I set out to confirm or correct them. On February 15, 1929, I trimmed all infested material off the tops of 10 shoulder-high loblollies, and on each tree, I installed an improved voile cage, plumped out by light wire hoops and supported by a tripod of gum poles. During the first flight of adult moths, early in March 1929, and during each flight thereafter, I inserted from 5 to 20 live moths in each of two or more infestation-free cages, leaving other cages without moths as checks. A week or so after I had inserted the moths and they had had time to lay eggs, I recovered the moths or their remains from the cages and then watched both treated and check cages for development and emergence of a new brood. My official diary for May 15, 1929, reads:

Inspected tipmoth cages; strong presumptive evidence, though not quite absolute proof, that there has been a complete life cycle since I inserted moths in cages 1-4 early in March. Second flight of year is at its height.

This is a photo of the cages that Wakeley used to determine the life cycle of tip moths that cause early damage to seedling stem elongation.

What kept proof from being absolute was the accidental infestation of one or two untreated check cages. I suspected either oviposition or foliage in contact with the cages or migration of larvae up the tree stems, as the source of the trouble. Accordingly, in 1930, I improved my technique still further. I made new cages, of voile above and unbleached muslin below, installed them with Tree Tanglefoot on the stem above and below the point of attachment, removed all twigs and foliage from contact with the cage walls, and made successive artificial infestations as in 1929.

I believe it was during the first artificial infesting of these cages in 1930 that Milt Miley, one of the Great Southern's notably astute foremen, came by on his way home from work and found me in difficulties. The twigs of the trees near the cages were full of freshly opened pupa cases, but I could find no adult moths.

"Why, Mr. Wakeley," Milt said, "with the wind blowing as hard as it is, the moths won't be in the trees. They'll be down in the grass. Here! Gimme your little bottle."

He dropped down on his knees and in almost no time he had all the fresh adult moths I needed. After I had inserted them in the cages, I said: "Milt, how'd you happen to know what a full-grown tip moth looks like? Most people I've talked to never have seen them."

"Well, sir, for a fact, they look so like that gray stuff around the bottom of the pine needles that most folks never notice them. But me, I got tired of something eatin' on our trees and me not knowing what it was. So I took home some twigs with them little wigglers in 'em" (the pupae are in fact motile)" and put 'em in a pan of water and tied my wife's dish-towel over 'em and made her wipe them with her apron until the moths come out."

It's a mistake to under-rate either the observation or the intelligence of good workers like Milt Miley. It took him to tell me the moths hid in the grass on windy days.

My official diary for 1930 contains this entry:

Monday, July 14, 1930 ... inspected the tip moth cages, which yielded convincing evidence at last of the short (6-8 week) life cycle of the moth.

I took down the last of the cages October 16, 1930, and published the study in Occasional Paper 45, in April 1935. We had to reissue the paper in 1941 to meet demand. The following excerpt from it gives the essence of the story as the Second Era tightening up of experimental procedure showed it.

The most clear-cut evidence of all was obtained from the second generation in the 1930 cages. Adults were obtained July 14, 1930, as the offspring of adults inserted May 14, 1930, in two separate cages. One of these cages had been free from all signs of tip moths and tip moth activity since January 12, 1930, and the other since July 4, 1929.

While the moths in these two cages were passing through their complete life cycle, seven check cages, of which two had contained moths of the first generation, remained absolutely free from moths of the second generation and from signs of their activity.

On the basis of the evidence obtained in this study, it may be concluded that the Nantucket tip moth has four successive generations per year on young pines of susceptible species in southeastern Louisiana.

There followed some comments on the bearing of these findings on planting policy, including the introduction of exotics having fewer than four flushes of growth a year. The devastating effects of tip moth on the Monterey pine planted in Florida by the St. Joe Paper Company in the early Fifties pretty well confirmed the soundness of this comment regarding exotics.

GROWTH OF THE STATION STAFF

High aspirations, a yeasty intellectual ferment, improved perspective and a better grasp of experimental procedure marked the Second Era. Not that high aspirations had been lacking before. Forbes was idealistic and enthusiastic to a fault, and my own youthful and innocent dreams were numerous and grandiose enough for 10 men. Too many of our early ambitions, however, were vague and unrealistic, as the first typescript annual investigative programs in the Station's "posterity file" plainly show. During the second era, we began to sense the difference between discrete studies and the galaxies of studies we now call "projects" and to shift our attention from saving the whole world to making our research sound.

Those of us already at the Station were learning much, both from our wealth of experimental material and from our past mistakes. New young recruits came from a greater number of schools and varied greatly in points of view. We recruited a leavening of older, experienced workers too. We read more. There was constant, untrammelled discussion—much more of it than the New Orleans Office, at least, enjoys today—among ourselves and with the growing numbers of professional visitors from this country and abroad.

These developments were timely. The era opened with good prospects, soon realized, of the passage of the McNary-McSweeney Act. Under this Act, the Station grew and grew right through the first years of the depression that started in 1929.

In calendar year 1927, the Station staff, professional and non-professional, permanent and non-permanent, in New Orleans and in the field, totalled 23. In 1928, the year of the South Pasture fire, it totalled 28. In 1932, the last year before the Nile-flood of New Deal emergency and relief funds simultaneously inundated and enriched the Station, the staff totalled 64.

Table 2—Composition of the Southern Station staff, 1928 and 1932

Agency	Class of employee	Number employed in 1928	Number employed in 1932
U.S. Forest Service	Professional, Director	1	1
	Professional, Principal	–	1
	Professional, Full Grade	–	3
	Professional, Associate	2	4
	Professional, Assistant	2	6
	Professional, Junior	4	16
	Professional, Agent	1	1
	Professional, Temporary Field Assistant	10	12
	Nonprofessional, field	1	1
	Nonprofessional, clerical	6	14
Bureau of Plant Industry	Professional, permanent	1	3
	Professional, Temporary Field Assistant	–	2
Total		28	64

Table 2, which summarizes by categories, the numbers of employees in 1928 and 1932, shows roughly the human resources with which the Station passed into and out of the second era. Only roughly, however. Counting heads, even by the categories of this table, does not assess their contents. Some of our 1927 or 1928 to 1932 recruits became justly famous later on, and a number of others contributed mightily to the Station's achievement and got all too little credit for their contributions. Our clerical employees in particular have had less recognition than they deserve.

Junior Foresters

An entry in my personal diary at Bogalusa, on July 1, 1927, chronicles the vanguard of the second era juniors as follows: "Verne Harper, Junior Forester just appointed here on his way to Starke. Quiet; nice chap." My personal diary for Saturday (we used to work Saturdays), June 18, 1932, reads: "Talked seed treatment and Station administration with Les Harper." I have added the underscore in transcription, as the subject is predictive. Early in the Third Era, Les became the Southern Station's first Division Chief of Forest Management, and now,

A distinguished group of important visitors, valued cooperators, and seasoned staff members near Sampson Lake Naval Stores Experimental Tract, Starke, FL, March 5, 1929. Left to right: F.I. (Pete) Righter, V.L. (Les) Harper, James Beal, Les Wyman, Perkins Coville, Dr. Clarence F. Korstian, Dr. Carl Hartley, and Paul Siggers.

of course, is Deputy Chief of the Forest Service, in charge of all the Service's research.

Junior Foresters recruited during the second era proper include: C.A. ("Al") Bickford, lately Biometrician for the Northeastern Station and since the summer of 1963, on the New York State College of Forestry staff; the late Roy A. Chapman, who had been my Temporary Field Assistant at Bogalusa in 1926; J.W. ("Jimmy") Cruikshank, who headed the Southeastern Forest Survey for many years; and Frank Heyward, the ex-architectural student who nearly became our first specialist in forest soils but left (the day after we got him his Kjeldah apparatus!) to become, briefly, State Forester of Georgia and then public relations specialist for Gaylord Container Corporation at Bogalusa.

They included T.A. ("Ted") Liefeld, for a time Officer-in-Charge at Lake City toward the end of that Research Center's inclusion in the Southern Station's territory. Ted resigned after a losing battle with H.L. Mitchell during (though only remotely connected with) World War II, to become one of the South's earlier consulting foresters.

Ralph M. ("Lindy") Lindgren was detailed to the Station August 1, 1928, by the old Bureau of Plant Industry, in a grade equivalent to Junior Forester, right after completing his Master's in plant pathology under Stakman at Minnesota. He resigned as Chief of the then Division of Wood Preservation at the Forest Products Laboratory on June 30, 1962. An account of his intervening career would fill many pages. His work on control of sap stain won the Station its first unqualified credit and acceptance, both here and abroad, and Lindy is one of those who generate episodes that grow into lively anecdotes and, ultimately, legends.

Also recruited as Junior Foresters before the end of 1932 were H.G. ("Mac") Meginnis (until the recent reorganization), Division Chief of Watershed Research at the Southeastern Station and the only Forest Service employee I have ever known to be reallocated directly from Junior Forester P-l to Silviculturist P-4; C.F. ("Ivy") Olsen, my planting assistant during the CCC period, who received the Carnegie Medal for his gallant but unsuccessful attempt to save A.L. MacKinney from drowning in 1938; J.G. ("Ted") Osborne, who succeeded Francis X. Schumacher as Biometrician at the Washington Office; R.R. ("Russ") Reynolds, who made the Crossett Research Center famous, invented "farm forties" (though some research purists hold this against him!), and won the Department's Superior Service

C.F. "Ivy" Olsen received the Carnegie Medal for his gallant attempt to save A.L. MacKiney from drowning in 1938. Ivy was a planting assistant to Wakeley during the CCC period.

Award; F.I. ("Pete") Righter, who has performed miracles of pine hybridization at Placerville, California but who has, alas, published all too little about them); Paul O. Rudolf, for years a pillar of strength at the Lake States Station, is one of the most scholarly of American Research foresters; A.R. ("Art") Spillers, now Associate Deputy Chief of the Service, in State and Private Forestry and P.R. ("Phil") Wheeler, who came to us from a forest reconnaissance job in Brazil, was the Coast Guard's Captain of the Port of New Orleans during World War II, and retired in 1962 as Division Chief of Forest Economics Research at the Southern Station.

These Junior Foresters of the second era were an able lot, but the Temporary Field Assistants of the same period rivaled them in talents, training and later accomplishments.

Temporary Field Assistants

Frank W. Bennett now has his own firm of consultants, F.W. Bennett and Associates, working out of Baton Rouge. W.C. ("Bill") Bramble is head of the Department of Forestry and Conservation at Purdue and very active in the Society of American Foresters. A. Chapman, Lindgren's first assistant in the sap stain research, has his own company, the Chapman Chemical Company, purveying Lignasan and other toxic substances; for a while Lindy was also a member of Chapman's firm. T.S. ("Ted") Coile, for a long time, taught forest soils at Duke University and is now a forest soils consultant. C.H. ("Hux") Coulter has for many years been State Forester in Florida, and is almost unique among State Foresters in his background of planting experience.

Lincoln ("Linc") Ellison, a man of rare research ability and even rarer personal qualities, was at the time of his tragic death, in an avalanche while skiing in 1958, Chief of the Division of Range Research at the Intermountain Station.

T.C. ("Tommy") Evans later obtained permanent appointment with the Southern Forest Survey at the Southern Station. Then, for many years, he was Biometrician at the Southeastern, left the Southeastern to succeed Ted Osborne as Biometrician in the Washington Office, and left Washington in turn to teach at Virginia Polytechnic Institute.

Ralph W. Hayes was a Temporary Field Assistant in the summers 1927 through 1930, at an age considerably past that of most field assistants, and after some years in the Indian Service. He and I published Louisiana State University, University Bulletin, Vol. 21, New Series, No. 3, Part 2, "Survival and early growth of planted southern pine in southeastern Louisiana", in May 1929. The bulletin was full of misprints and required the attachment of a letter-size, single-spaced errata sheet and cost me a sharp reprimand from the Washington Office, where it was not known that Ralph had corrected the galley proof at Baton Rouge while arranging his young daughter's funeral. The bulletin is nevertheless invaluable for its map of the Great Southern Lumber Company's earlier plantations and for its list of the geographic sources of seed of all but a few of that Company's plantations from 1920 through 1928. For many years after this publication, Ralph was Head of the School of Forestry at L.S.U.

George H. Hepting, long-time Chief of the Division of Forest Disease Research at the Southeastern Station and now the Department's specialist in forest disease problems, was a Bureau of Plant Forestry Temporary Field Assistant at the Southern in 1932. C.S. ("Clint") Herrick, now in charge of employee development and training for Region 8 in Atlanta, was a Forest Service Assistant at the Southern that same year. So, in 1931 and 1932, was M.A. ("Morrie") Huberman, who was my nursery research assistant on permanent appointment during the CCC period, and whose ambition and drive finally led him through the Washington Office to the FAO, first in Rome, Italy and then in Mexico.

Frank Kaufert, a Bureau of Plant Industry Field Assistant in 1931 and a Forest Service Field Assistant in 1932, is now Director of the School of Forestry at the University of Minnesota. Franklin G. Liming, long in charge of the Northern Ozarks Research Center of the Central States Station and now in Washington handling international exchanges of tree seed for research purposes, was also a Bureau of Plant Industry Assistant in 1931. T.E. Maki (generally "Waldy" but still "Tenyo" to a few old friends) is now Hoffman Distinguished Professor of Forest Management and head of the Department of Silviculture, School of Forestry, at North Carolina State College. H.E. ("Herb") Ochsner is Assistant Regional Forester in charge of Timber Management in Region 9.

Ralph Hayes served as Director of LSU's School of Forestry until the late 1950s.

Putnam became the leading authority on the silviculture of southern bottomland hardwoods. He was referred to as "Mr. Hardwoods."

Somewhat older and more experienced than any of our Field Assistants except Ralph Hayes was Eric Östlin, a Swedish forester and something of a specialist in mensuration, who was on temporary appointment with us in 1927 during a period of study in this country. As I recall, he was here on a Scandinavian-American fellowship.

John ("Put") Putnam was Lentz's field assistant on the bottomland hardwood reconnaissance in 1928 and I believe on the first Southern Forest Survey in 1931. He came to us with unique and valuable experience acquired in logging a hardwood tract or tracts, owned by his family, received permanent appointment as a Junior Forester in 1931, later did for the Stoneville Research Center what Russ Reynolds did for the Crossett Center, and has long been *the* hardwood authority for both the Station and Region 8.

Theodore ("Ted") Scheffer, a quiet man, Temporary Field Assistant for the Bureau of Plant Industry in 1930 and 1931 and one of its Agents at the Station in 1932, has since had a long and productive career at the Forest Products Laboratory.

A.F. ("Art") Verrall, Paul Siggers' Bureau of Plant Industry Field Assistant in brown-spot research at Bogalusa in 1932 (a master of many techniques, producer of free-hand sections that rivalled microtome sections and the only man I ever knew who both owned and played a gold flute!) returned to do years of excellent research at Gulfport on the interrelations of house construction, paint problems and decay and to head up vast Army and Navy studies on ammunition-box decay and on deterioration of wood structures in the tropics. He became in June 1964, Chief of the Division of Forest Disease Research Forest Station headquarters in New Orleans, he is now Principal Pathologist, specializing again in products pathology.

An admirable lot, these Junior Foresters and Temporary Field Assistants of the second era. During the past 30 years I have forgotten the schools at which most of them got their undergraduate training[1], though originally I had this information about them all. No matter. They came from many different schools. There was a preponderance of University of Michigan foresters among them; Demmon, who was Director at the time, felt (and justifiably, as events showed) that he could depend on his fellow alumni from Ann Arbor. But California, Cornell, Georgia, Iowa State, Louisiana State University, Michigan State, Minnesota, Syracuse, Yale and several others were represented also and the variety of doctrines, enthusiasms, interests, specialties and techniques these recent graduates brought in created an ideal intellectual climate within our rapidly expanding organization.

Through the work assigned to them and from sheer force of numbers, these Junior Foresters and Temporary Field Assistants carried the main load of the Station's research routine—plot measurements and remeasurements, quadrat counts, gum weighing, germination tests, experimental treatments, note-taking, compilation of data and office computations. Yet, permanent and temporary employees alike, they also initiated research—some of it of great value—to an extent that is strictly against regulations for men of comparable employment grades today and that probably would have been frowned upon by the Civil Service Commission and perhaps by our own Washington Office, even then. We didn't care. If a man could find out something portent to an undertaking, we encouraged him to do so, regardless of his age or grade. If a Temporary Field Assistant knew a better technique than the Director did, he told the Director.

---

[1] In passing, at least two of the Junior Foresters and at least nine of the Temporary Field Assistants I have named earned the Ph.D. degree after serving at the Station during the second era. I have neither the information nor the time to figure out why four and a half times as many Field Assistants as Junior Foresters went on to acquire the doctorate, but it's interesting speculation. Which came first, the hen or the egg? And to what extent was early marriage involved?

For Romans in Rome's quarrel
Spared neither goods nor gold
Nor son nor wife nor limb nor life
In the brave days of old.
Then none was for a party.
Then all were for the State.
Then the rich man helped the poor
And the poor man loved the great.
Then lands were fairly portioned.
Then spoils were fairly sold.
The Romans were like brothers
In the brave days of old!

Conditions have by no means deteriorated to the stage Macauley describes in the next line of "Horatius"—"Now, Roman is to Roman more hateful than a foe"—but it's a long time since a Temporary Field Assistant has said to the Director: "Mitch," (or "Phil" or "Walt") "a hell of a lot better way to do that is thus and so." Today's Field Assistant submits his suggestion "through channels!"

Old Hands

Although many of the Junior Foresters and Field Assistants I have mentioned did good work and showed great promise before 1933, most of them made their principal contributions later. From 1928 through 1933, it was the leavening of more experienced workers who mainly developed and guided the Station's program.

Not counting Forbes, the first Director, who had left in July to organize the Allegheny Station at Philadelphia, there were six of us relatively old hands at the Southern Station in the fall of 1927—Barrett, Demmon, Harper, Wahlenberg, Wyman and myself. (I say "old"; I was 25!) There had been a seventh, L.J. ("Doc") Pessin, but he had resigned June 14, 1927, to work on cotton-wilt root-rot at the Texas Agricultural Experiment Station. Wahlenberg had come in on April 1 from his prior assignment on nursery and planting research at the Savenac

Southern Forest Experiment Station professionals in 1932. Left to right, front row: L.J. Pessin, E.W. Gremmer, V.L. Harper, E.L. Demmon, G.H. Lentz, Lenthall Wyman, P.C. Wakeley, W.G. Wahlenberg. Second row: W.E. Bond, C.F. Olsen, R.B. Craig, P.V. Siggers, J.A. Putnam, V.B. Davis, A.R. Spillers, H.G. Meginnis, R.K. Winters. Back row: Henry Bull, Allen Bickford, F.K. Beyer, Ellery Foster, J.A. Lubbe, P.R. Wheeler, J.W. Cruikshank, E.B. Faulks, R.R. Reynolds, M.M. Lehrbas.

Nursery in Montana, where he had already established his reputation as an imaginative and thorough worker and had picked up Pessin's work at McNeill before Pessin left. And Harper, who had arrived even later than Wahlenberg on July 1, 1927, was not a very old "old hand" in either age or experience.

Barrett was transferred to the new Central States Station on December 15, 1928. Pessin, disillusioned regarding research on root-rot in Texas, returned to the Southern Station June 1, 1928. Wahlenberg resigned March 5, 1929 to take a position at the then Eddy Tree Breeding Station at Placerville, California but returned to the Southern Station in 1930, disillusioned by the Tree Breeding Station's Director, Lloyd Austin.

Then, in addition to rerecruiting Pessin and Wahlenberg (and though losing Barrett to the Central States Station), we acquired a round dozen of relatively experienced men.

W.E. ("Walt") Bond, who had been Assistant State Forester of Texas, came to us as Forest Economist in 1930.

Henry ("Hank") Bull, specialist in pine thinnings, a substantial joint contributor with Putnam to early dendrological and silvical research in hardwoods and a nearly flawless technical writer, came to us as Assistant Silviculturist after professional training at Yale and some work with, as I remember, the Connecticut Agricultural Experiment Station. His long illness and ultimate death from emphysema was one of the great tragedies of the Station and the whole forestry profession.

R.B. ("Ron") Craig joined the staff as Assistant Forest Economist in 1932; his main assignment, until his eventual transfer to the Washington Office, was on forest taxation studies.

E.W. ("Gene") Gemmer, who had worked under Station direction but on Region 7's payroll for 4 years, joined the Station's regular staff as Assistant Silviculturist in 1930.

M.M. ("Mark") Lehrbas joined the staff as Assistant Forest Economist in 1931 and plunged almost at once into the field direction of the burgeoning Southern Forest Survey. He was later made Director of the Goldenrod Rubber Project at Waynesboro, Georgia during World War II and I served under him there, Snedecor in hand, as Statistician of the Project by delegated authority of the Secretary of Agriculture. After the War, Mark became the first Division Chief of the Forest Utilization Service—now Forest Utilization Research, a subdivision of "R.E.E.P."—in the New Orleans Office.

G.H. ("Gus") Lentz, who had served as Special Investigator in charge of the 1927-1928 bottom-land hardwood reconnaissance while on leave of absence from the College of Forestry at Syracuse, accepted permanent appointment at the Station as Silviculturist early in 1930. I remember that on his return to New Orleans, I was still complaining about the decrepit Model-T Ford (70,000 miles on its intermittently

Mark Lehrbas, a University of Idaho graduate, began to work for the Forest Service on the Ouachita NF in Arkansas.

functioning speedometer; 8 miles to the gallon; maximum speed below 20 miles an hour) in which I had made a 1,200-mile nursery survey in November 1929; we had then got a turn-in allowance of $12.50 on the Model-T and the dealer from whom we got the new car in exchange had to tow the old one away from my house with a wrecker. Gus, who had an aggressive, dominating disposition didn't propose to have a mere Assistant Silviculturist like myself out-gripe him and said: "I bet it wasn't as beat up as the Ford Put and I used in the hardwoods back in 1928!"

"Doggone it, Gus," I told him truthfully and unanswerably, "it is the *same* Ford!"

N.T. ("Nick") Mirov served a brief term as Assistant Silviculturist on the permanent staff at Starke, on naval stores research, but I didn't meet him then. I first met him during a return engagement at Lake City in 1942, when he was working on the War Emergency "acid stimulation" project; one of the delights of my assignment to Lake City that year was Nick's wonderful doodles—voluptuous mermaids hatching out of dragons' eggs and the like. Nick is, I believe, the only Southern Station alumnus besides Les Harper to hold the Department's Distinguished Service Award, granted in Nick's case for comprehensive analysis and classification of pine oleoresins.

Paul V. Siggers was assigned to the Station by the Bureau of Plant Industry as Associate Pathologist December 1, 1928, to pick up and expand the work on brown-spot needle disease of longleaf pine that I had started immediately following the South Pasture fire at Bogalusa. Paul had no statistical background whatsoever but made up for this lack to an astonishing extent by virtue of sound pathological training, unflagging effort, rigorous and original thought and cross checking of results by repeated and independent approaches to the problem at hand. His researches on brown spot and on fusiform rust were monuments, not mere milestones, in the Station's development.

He was one of the most precise technical writers I have ever known and a superbly constructive critic of the writings of others. A lovable man and notable for economy of speech. The first day he called at the office just before he reported for duty, Doc Pessin was the only member of the professional staff in town. Doc talked to Paul at length about pathology, ecology, physiology, and on the way to lunch, about literature, art and world politics and elicited rapt attention and polite smiles and nods, but no comments. Finally, as they neared the cafeteria, Doc sensed that Paul was at last about to speak.

Paul did. He said: "This the place?"

A.E. ("Wack") Wackerman, afterwards for many years Professor of Forest Economics at Duke, came to the Station from the Crossett Company in 1932, as Forester. Both before leaving Crossett and after coming to New Orleans, he played an important part in arranging the very effective cooperative agreement between the Crossett Company and the Station, whereby we obtained the Crossett Experimental Forest, established the original Crossett experiment in all-aged management and launched Russ Reynolds on his career.

Wackerman left Crossett Lumber Company due the cutbacks resulting from the Depression. He spent many years at Duke University teaching harvesting.

R.K. ("Bob") Winters, now Director of Foreign Forestry Services in the Washington Office, came to us as Assistant Silviculturist in 1930. Although most of his later work with the Station was in connection with the Southern Forest Survey and particularly with sampling procedures, much of his time at first was devoted to hardwood dendrology and silvics. Next after Averell, he probably contributed most to the Station's photographic work during the second era and he illustrated with excellent photos the official file copy of Putnam and Bull's "The trees of the bottomlands of the Mississippi River Delta Region."

Dr. E.A. Ziegler, ex-Director of the Pennsylvania Forest Academy at Mont Alto, came to us in 1929 (when that unique institution ended its independent existence) to head up our newly undertaken research in forest taxation, cost of timber-growing and the like. He resigned September 30, 1931 to direct the Pennsylvania Forest Research Institute for 6 years and from there went, in 1937, to join the staff of the recently organized School of Forestry at the University of Florida. I question whether our present economics staff would rate Dr. Ziegler as a trained professional economist and I can't truthfully say that he exerted a great formative influence on the Station's program, though he may have contributed more than I saw from my place in another Division. Certainly his studies, such as that he made with Art Spillers, one of the "roofer" industry in Alcorn County, Mississippi were exploratory only and though glowingly presented in the Station's Annual Reports, have left little trace. As his maturity, his previous career of teaching and of civic activities in a small, stable community and his combination of integrity and charm made him personally influential, especially among the younger members of the staff. It was good to have him here at this particular stage in the Station's development.

Lastly, to take over the budding Southern Forest Survey in 1932, and later the whole Division of Forest Economics Research, came Inman ("Cap") Eldredge, certainly the most colorful employee the Station ever had and among the most colorful the American profession can claim.

He was a South Carolinian by birth, a graduate of Dr. Schenk's exotic Biltmore School of Forestry, and in 1909, had become Supervisor of the Ocala and Choctawhatchee National Forests—the latter now—Eglin Air Force Base. He had worked in California and then in the Washington Office. It was in Washington that he had discouraged Raphael Zon's frequent scrounging of a "pipeful" of tobacco in the huge calabash pipe that Zon kept for the purpose and that held enough to fill three times over the briar pipe in which Zon actually smoked what he borrowed. The story is told that Eldredge dosed the last of the tobacco in his own can with finely cutup rubber bands just before Zon came in and filled his calabash from it. Later Eldredge, himself unseen, heard Zon remark in the men's room: "This young fellow Eldritch ve have brought in from the Vest is a very smart young man, but he smokes the vorst tobacco of any forester I have ever met!"

I.F. "Cap" Eldredge retired from the Southern Station in 1944, but in 1956 was awarded the Gifford Pinchot medal for his contributions to forestry. Eldredge was only the third individual to receive the award.

Cap's fund of humor was inexhaustible. If it was sometimes a shade robust (as when, in the summer of 1934, in his capacity as Acting Director, it amused him to send me to Washington for 2 weeks on a $3 per diem while he toured the small towns in the Station territory on $5!), it was always good-natured and usually scintillating.

It was said of Cap that he so loved to trade horses that he would trade them even if he neither had nor wanted a horse. This estimate of him may have grown out of an episode during his service with the famous Forestry Regiment in France during World War I.

The story goes that some "remounts" were obtained to replace the worn-out draft horses with which the Regiment was logging under the jealous eyes of the French foresters and were to be shared equally between Cap's company and another. Cap and the captain of the rival company had their horse-flesh-canny teamsters tether the remounts in order from best to worst and tossed a coin to see who would get the odd-numbered horses. Cap lost; his were to be the slightly inferior even-numbered beasts.

At that moment, out of sight around the stable, a fist was heard to smack a jaw and someone yelled "Fight!" The other captain, all the non-coms, and all the men except Cap and his teamsters ran to separate the combatants and conduct them to the guardhouse. After order had been restored and the other captain had rejoined Cap, Cap's team led away the even-numbered horses—and somehow got much the better half of the remounts!

I first met Cap at Fargo, Georgia in the summer of 1926, when he was just beginning to organize the vast holdings of what was then the Superior Pine Products Company. From Fargo, in 1931, he supplied the Station with the famous lot of slash pine seed carried in the records as "Old Faithful"; a portion of it that had been kept in cold storage germinated 84 percent in 1962. Cap use to boast that this seed was extracted in the only mahogany-lined seed extractory ever operated in the South. It was mahogany-lined too and had stained-glass windows high up under the roof. It was an ancient Pullman car that had been made over into a rolling bunkhouse by the Superior Pine Products Company. Cap had replaced the bunks with wire-bottomed racks, filled the racks with slash pine cones, opened the stained glass ventilators and left the car on a railroad siding in the sun till the cones opened. Then he hauled the car over a few miles of rough logging railroad to jar the seeds out of the cones and swept the seeds down the aisle, into the lavatory and into burlap sacks hooked under the hole in the floor where the toilet had been. Ingenious man, Cap.

Seeds from Eldredge's 1931 collection were tested many times; the last was after 50 years of storage. The results were published in a Forest Science article (Barnett and Vozzo 1985).

Forest Sci., Vol. 31, No. 2, 1985, pp. 316–320
Copyright 1985, by the Society of American Foresters

Viability and Vigor of Slash and Shortleaf Pine Seeds After 50 Years of Storage

James P. Barnett and J. A. Vozzo

ABSTRACT. Viability of slash and shortleaf pine seeds was 66 and 25 percent, respectively, after 50 years of cold storage. Evaluations of leachate conductance, chromosomal aberrations, and seedling development indicated some loss of vigor over the storage period, but probably not enough to affect adversely the genetic makeup of the next generation. FOREST SCI. 31:316–320.

ADDITIONAL KEY WORDS. *Pinus elliottii, Pinus echinata,* germination, seed vigor, seed longevity, cytological change, chromosomal aberrations, leachate conductance.

Cap came to the Station as Principal Forest Economist March 15, 1932 to head the Southern Forest Survey. At first, I understood his pay exceeded that of the Director and if it did, I have no doubt (knowing Cap), that he used the fact to "pull rank" and get what he wanted when be wanted it. But his wisdom and experience were invaluable assets to the Station for many long years. Also, there was never a dull moment in his presence, for as a raconteur, he was unrivalled.

The "leavening of older, experienced workers" that I have mentioned improved the Station's performance in immediately obvious ways—by refining familiar techniques and introducing new ones, for example, and by defining more sharply the problems to be solved and designing more rigorous experiments to solve them. Looking back, though, it seems to me that these seasoned workers—and an important part of their seasoning had been derived from experience in publishing research—made their greatest contributions, not in the techniques they introduced, but in attitude.

Wahlenberg, for instance, though one of the most charitable of men, was no softie where investigative integrity was concerned. The fire, grazing and longleaf reproduction study at McNeill ultimately became his responsibility and after a year or two at it he said: "If we had worked one-tenth as hard to verify what turned out the way we thought it would as we have to explain away the results, we didn't expect, this would have been a much more honest piece of research." That the results of the McNeill study ever got into print, was due entirely to Wally's re-evaluation of the data that had been taken before he inherited the McNeill assignment, his own bolstering up of the study with supplementary sampling and additional plots and his statesmanlike negotiations with Greene, our original cooperator with the Bureau of Animal Industry. Greene had developed an acute antagonism to the Station and all its works but nevertheless finally coauthored U.S. Department Agriculture Tech. Bul. 683, "Effects of fire and cattle grazing on longleaf pine lands as studied at McNeill, Miss". (1929) with Wally and H.R. Reed.

On November 12, 1930, during an inspection trip from the Washington Office, Ed Munns made a comment on our loblolly spacing Station at Bogalusa that was as caustic as Wahlenberg's on the McNeill study, and even more instructive.

At 8 years in the field, the plantation spaced 6 by 6 feet and especially that spaced 8 by 8 feet, already showed better diameter growth than the 5 by 5, but the 5 by 5 was conspicuously less bushy, had recovered much better from tip-moth injury and showed the beginnings of self-pruning. We were proud of these results, but Ed brushed them contemptuously aside. He made us admit that we had tried the 5 by 5 and the 8 by 8, as well as the 6 by 6 that Hawley and Hawes recommended for white pine in New England, in hopes of hitting upon just the right spacing for the cooperator on whose lands we had planted.

"The 5 by 5 looks better than the others, sure," said Ed. "How do you know the company won't go to 4 by 4 and stagnate the stand before it reaches merchantable pulpwood size? You've done nothing to show the possible danger of that. You ought to have made your close spacing 4 by 4 instead of 5 by 5, and you ought to have made your wide one 10 by 10 instead of 8 by 8; you'd have gotten results even quicker than you actually have and would have had a broader basis for generalization."

"Always," he added, "extend your experimental treatments beyond the extremes of present economic feasibility, in both directions. That's the way to get the essential biologic facts and to be informed in time to cope with economic change." This precept was the making of many of my own experiments later on and, directly or indirectly, of many Station studies in fields other than my own. It is as sound today as it was in 1929.

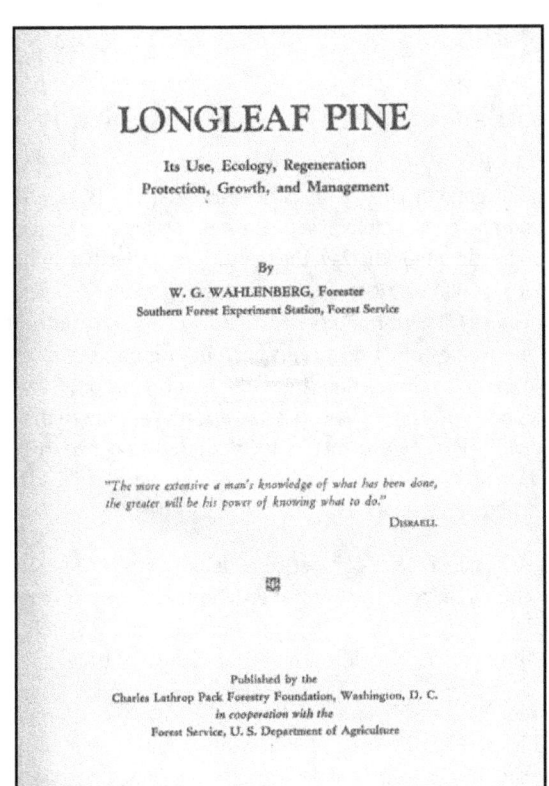

W.G. Wahlenberg authored two major books—one on longleaf pine 1946 and one on loblolly pine in 1960. These books provided a valuable reference by compiling available knowledge in a single source (Wahlenberg 1946, 1960).

BALANCE AND DIVERSIFICATION

During the Primitive Era, we had all been pretty much routine pine silviculturists, slightly tinctured with old-style, nonstatistical mensuration. During the Era of Expansion and Recognition, we became, by recruitment and to some extent by self-help, a much better balanced group, with specialized experience or formal professional training in botany, ecology, economics, erosion, control, hardwood management, physiology, plant pathology, statistics, and utilization. With a much stronger as well as a much larger staff, the Station was able to extend research into several new fields.

During his first brief period of service with the Station, Pessin ("Doc" or "L.J.") had been thrown into the breach left by Hadley's resignation and been given the McNeill grazing, burning and reproduction study to handle as his main assignment. The assignment was "justified" in the Annual Report ("annual investigative program") by no better an argument than that, as a botanist, he would be especially qualified to deal with small plants. (His height—he was 5 feet 1 inch or "One inch taller than Napoleon," to quote one of his favorite statements—would have been as valid a justification.) Doc kept the quadrant counts faithfully and accurately up to date and contributed an ingenious improvement to our record forms. He got on poorly, however, with our cooperator, Greene, at the McNeill Branch Experiment Station, but then, Greene was hard to get on with, anyway.

On his return to the Station from Texas in July 1928, Pessin was assigned to the ecological studies for which he had been hired in the first place.

None of us had the temerity to suggest the outlines of this field to Pessin. We—and Washington—stood rather in awe of his training; he was the first man we got who had the Ph.D. Doc was modest about his degree and made no claim to knowing much about forestry, though he had begun his college career as a forestry student at the University of Georgia. (His Ph.D. dissertation had been on the ecology of the resurrection fern, that grows on tree trunks and branches and when his first boy, Jaques, grew old enough to talk, Doc boasted that the first words he learned were the name of this fern, *Polypodium polypodioides*.) He told Ed Munns he knew nothing of forestry and Ed told him not to worry; he'd "absorb it by osmosis."

Doc was an eager, earnest, alert, widely informed and indefatigable man. It is interesting to speculate as to what he might have done had he had some statistical background and more experience as a team worker (temperamentally, although amiable and cooperative to a degree, he was a "lone wolf" in his approach to research) and had been directed and had had his studies and publications fitted into a coordinated program and planned and reviewed as would be the case today. As it was, numbers of the experiments, collections, compilations, arboreta and other enterprises he undertook turned out

poorly or came to naught, to his eventual discredit. The circumstances of the time, which seemed to glow so rosily in 1928, proved in the last analysis, to have been adverse to Dr. Pessin.

Doc has received altogether too little credit for improving the Station's contacts with scientists at Tulane University and Newcomb College. Among these were Dr. William Penfound and Dr. Miriam Bomhard, with whom Doc joined to found the New Orleans Botanical Society and to revitalize the moribund New Orleans Academy of Sciences. The Station benefited greatly for several years from participation in these two organizations; Miriam Bomhard later became a Forest Service employee and did notable work under Dayton in Washington and my own Puerto Rican trip in 1938 owes any success it may have had to the good offices of the then President of the Academy, Dr. Ernest Carroll Faust.

Pessin gave a tremendous impetus to the Station library, both through his outspoken wrath and horror at the paucity of our collection and through his own selection of botanical and physiological texts, numbers of which still grace our shelves today. On the whole, he shopped adroitly as well as conscientiously for books. It seemed to me, though, that he did have one curious weakness in this regard. If he discovered a new title before anyone else, it was the best as well as the latest thing out, but if someone else discovered it first and called it to his attention, it was rarely worth the paper it was printed on!

Pessin's Competition-Density Study

One of Doc's major studies was unique in every way. It was not, in our current jargon, "practice-oriented." In fact, it had absolutely no conceivable practical usefulness of any kind, as it is questionable whether the conditions under which he conducted it had ever occurred during the previous existence of the Upper Coastal Plain or will ever occur again. Yet it drove home to the very hilt Ed Munns' precept of going beyond feasible economic limits and it gave those of us who followed it a deeper insight into the behavior of longleaf pine than any "practical" study we ever made. Incidentally, it opened in 1932, the Service research career of one of the Forest Service's truly great scientists, the late Lincoln Ellison.

This study was Doc's "competition-density study." He laid it out in the Great Southern Lumber Company's South Pasture at Bogalusa, just south of the 1928 burn and immediately east of the fungicide spray plots I had established in 1928.

The study area had been open hog range till Red Bateman fenced it in 1921. The old-growth timber had been turpentined for 2 years before logging—that is, in 1918 and 1919. There had been a good seed crop in 1918, but the seedlings from this crop had been wiped out while still in the cotyledon stage, when the needle and grass rough under the old trees had been burned early in 1919 to protect the turpentine faces and cups. There was virtually no seed crop in

Lincoln Ellison left the Station, moved to the West, and became a charter member of the Society of Range Management. He was Chief of Range Management in the Intermountain Forest & Range Experiment Station when killed in a snow avalanche in 1958.

1919, and we have good evidence that fewer than 10 seedlings per acre survived from the 1918 and earlier crops.

The area was logged in the fall of 1920. That was the year of the all-time bumper crop of longleaf pine seed. Red Bateman and his woods crew, armed with wash tubs and garden rakes, collected 3,000 pounds of longleaf seed from the ditches along the Bogalusa-Franklinton highway that fall and Red told me that the Company had to put sandboxes on the logging locomotives in South Pasture because the wheels crushed so much oily seed on the rails that they just spun unless sanded.

Austin Cary had persuaded the Company to reburn about 1,500 acres in South Pasture in September 1920 to prepare the ground for the seed from the heavy crop of cones.

The area Doc chose for his competition-density study was within the burn suggested by Cary and in a patch logged and steam-skidded at the peak of the 1920 seedfall. Forty acres at this location averaged 400,000 seedlings per acre in 1932, at the start of their twelfth growing season. These were the survivors (after terrific annual brown-spot epidemics had taken their toll) of unimaginably greater numbers of seedlings that had become established during the winter of 1920-21. None of the 12-year-old seedlings was more than 3 inches high, and the modal height was about 1/2 inch.

In this amazing stand of natural reproduction, Doc Pessin laid out two series of 200-seedling measurement plots. In size, these plots were in multiples of 2 milacres, as required, and each plot was surrounded by an isolation strip 6.6 feet wide. Each series of these measurement plots and their isolation

strips Doc and Linc Ellison thinned down during the summer of 1932, to densities of 100,000 seedlings per acre; 50,000 per acre; 25,000; 15,000; 10,000; 5,000 and 1,000. At the highest density, there were 100 seedlings in a 6.6- by 6.6-foot square and at the lowest the seedlings were 6.6 feet apart, at square spacing. Practically all the seedlings left in the plots were of the modal size, 1/2-inch high.

From one set of plots at the seven different densities, Doc and Linc removed all grass and weeds and Doc kept them removed for the next 5 years. In the other series, grass and weeds were left in place. The seedlings in both series of plots were kept relatively free from brown spot for 5 years by frequent spraying with Bordeaux mixture.

At the end of the 5 years, the 16-year-old seedlings, in the 1,000-per-acre plot without grass, were about 8 feet high. At the opposite extreme of experimental treatment, the seedlings at 100,000 per acre with grass in place were only about 0.8 feet high. Those on plots of intermediate densities were of intermediate heights. Instead of a straightline relationship, however, there was a sharp break in the curve at 10,000 trees per acre; at densities greater than this, height growth had been meager. All seedlings on all plots, of course, had originated from the same seed crop and had been within a fraction of an inch of the same height when 11 to 12 years old. Doc closed the study at this point and published the 3-year results in *Ecological Monographs* 8 (1): 115-149, 1938.

When he closed the study he stopped spraying the plots. The seedlings at the lower densities and above 2 or 3 feet in height were above brown-spot danger despite the inoculum all around them and continued to grow well, though at rates

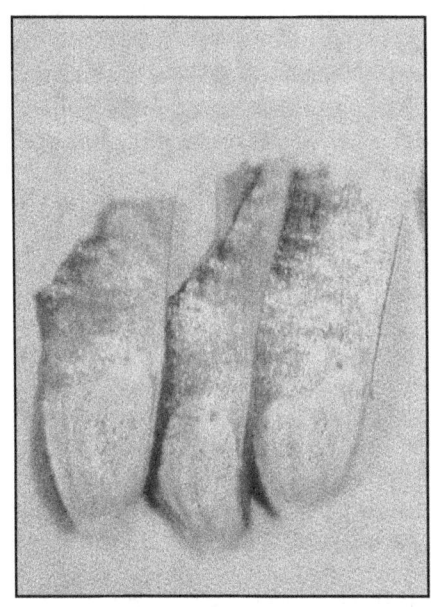

Longleaf pine seeds are the largest of the southern pines, rich in lipids, and are sought by birds and rodents.

determined to a great extent, by the numbers of trees per acre. The seedlings at densities of 10,000 or more were below the safe level in height, promptly became infected and mostly died. Today the 1,000-per-acre plots are beautiful pole stands, with trees 60 or 70 feet high. A few seedlings on the 100,000-per-acre plots have finally overcome competition and infection and have grown several feet in height, and a very few survive but are, at age 44, still less than 2 feet high.

Nobody could dispute this study's being "ecological." Further than that, it is hard to classify. Epithets applied to it have ranged from "pure," "basic," and "fundamental," through "academic" and "impractical" to "useless" and "asinine." It brought the Station recognition from readers of *Ecological Monographs*, but one dreads to think what a Congressional Investigative Committee might have made of it. Few other studies we have been able to show them have charmed foreign visitors so much; it is still a revelation to pathologists because of the height-susceptibility relationship manifested when spraying ceased and for some reason that I have never fathomed, New Zealanders in all walks of life have especially admired it. Personally, although I should feel obliged to veto its like today, I am very glad that Doc made it during the exuberance of the second era. I know my longleaf pine is the better for it.

Poisoning Scrub Oaks

One other "ecological" or "physiological" exploit of Pessin's deserves special mention, though it carries over into the Third Era.

In 1929, I had conceived the notion of poisoning scrub oaks on planting sites and had treated five scrub oaks apiece, near the Upper Coburn's Creek Plantations at Bogalusa on August 8, with ethyl mercury acetate 2%, ethyl mercury chloride 2%, ammoniacal arsenious oxide approximately 10%, "Fungimors" 2% and undiluted "Nekyan," applied in holes bored at the root collar with a bit and brace. I had selected the five chemicals with virtually no knowledge of chemistry and with entirely too little literature search. One chemical, I forget which, caused partial killing, but not enough to release planted trees effectively and the bit and brace involved excessive labor. I had other, more promising, enterprises to occupy my time and dropped the attempt to poison scrub oaks, but during my initial flush of enthusiasm, I had discussed the idea with Doc.

He was much better qualified than I was to tackle this particular problem and he started with a rapid but fairly comprehensive literature search. As a result of the literature search, he tried, among other reagents, sodium arsenate, and it worked. He published the results in Occasional Paper 102, 1942, "Recommendations for poisoning scrub oaks and other undesirable trees", and it at once became the best seller among the Station's publications. It gained the Station much credit (though of course at the cost of some jests about killing trees instead of growing them) and did much to counteract a certain reputation for impracticality that Doc had acquired.

Removing undesirable, poor-quality hardwoods on pine sites became necessary practice for establishing pine plantations on many upland sites.

As I recall, the paper was reissued not once, but several times. Though Ammate, 2,4-D and 2,4,5-T have long since replaced the dangerous sodium arsenate except under very special conditions, we still get a call now and then for Doc's original contribution and take xerox copies of the latest version to answer these requests. And Doc produced this best-seller on his own initiative, without the guidance and support of Project Leader, Division Chief and Editor that he would have had in later years. Or of Problem Selection and Problem Analysis, either.

The Bottom-Land Hardwood Survey

Even before the South Pasture fire and Doc Pessin's return to commence ecological research in 1928, the Station had begun another new venture, the Bottom-land Hardwood Survey.

Except for an inconsequential tupelo-gum volume, growth and yield study completed by Hadley, shortly after my arrival in 1924, the Station had done no work in hardwoods. Our official stand was that we had insufficient funds to conduct adequate research on the far more widely distributed and important southern pines, and that it could be folly to dilute our research effort by extending it to hardwoods. My understanding is that this strategy was dictated by Earl Clapp, then Assistant Chief in charge of the Branch of Research. I seem to recall, also, that it finally boomeranged, in that Congress, instead of appropriating additional funds for hardwoods as Clapp had hoped, earmarked some of our meager pine funds for hardwood research.

Putnam quickly became the leading authority on bottomland hardwood silviculture. His work is recognized for its excellence.

Demand for work on the valuable bottom-land hardwoods became more insistent, however, and by 1927 cooperative funds were negotiated. Those promised by the State of Mississippi failed to materialize, but the Louisiana Department of Forestry contributed some $5,000 for a survey of Delta hardwood resources, conditions and utilization in that State. G.H. Lentz and John Putnam began the survey in the spring of 1928 in one of our original 1924 Model-T Ford cars, U.S.D.A. license 653.

It would have been hard to recruit a better team for the job. Gus Lentz, who came to us December 10, 1927 from the New York State College of Forestry at Syracuse, was an intensely practical man, fairly bursting with energy and self confidence, and presented a favorable attitude toward the Station throughout the Southern hardwood industry. Put had spent some years logging family hardwood holdings, was a hardwood enthusiast to his marrow and even in 1928, probably knew the bottomland types better than any other professional forester in the South.

Gus and Put's 1928 reports on the Hardwood Survey and Putnam and Bull's reverently written, "The trees of the bottomlands of the Mississippi River Delta region" (1932), which was a further outcome of the initial work, were far superior to and far more effective than the reports on the old 1924-25 "Extensive Surveys" of southern pines. The typescript reports on the Extensive Surveys were typical products of the Primitive Era and reached few people outside the staff of the Station. The Station staff and ex-Director Forbes used them primarily as a rather inadequate foundation for U.S. Department Agriculture Tech. Bul. 204, "Timber growing and logging and turpentining practices in the Southern Pine Region." The results of the Hardwood Survey, by contrast, reached many influential people. "The trees of the bottomlands of the Mississippi River Delta region" won the admiration of a wide and varied audience. Certain master copies were beautifully illustrated with photographs by Bob Winters and the originally unnumbered paper was ultimately reissued, in a larger run, as Occasional Paper 27. In due time,

the Hardwood Survey of 1928 led to the establishment of the Station's bottomland hardwood Research Center and present Hardwoods Laboratory at Stoneville, Mississippi.

One anecdote concerning Gus and Put's 1928 hardwood survey seems, to me, to deserve perpetuation.

In 1914, Wilbur R. Mattoon, then in the Branch of Research, established two plots in a fine stand of medium-sized baldcypress near Skidder Landing, Belle Isle, St, Martin Parish, Louisiana to learn whether cypress knees actually served a useful function as "breathing organs" or in any other way. He numbered all the cypresses on both plots with brass tags, cut off all the knees on one plot and left the other plot with knees intact to serve as a check.

Shortly thereafter, Matty was metamorphosed into an extension specialist and had to abandon his research. He was still curious about the function of cypress knees, however, and when he heard about Gus and Put's survey, he sent them the data on the plots and asked them to follow up on the experiment.

Gus and Put set out with a colorful character named Captain Forgey of the Jeanerette Lumber Company and a laborer to relocate the plots, which Forgey had helped Mattoon establish. The water was high in the bottoms; for quite a bit of the way, it was waist-deep on Gus Lentz, which meant it was nearly

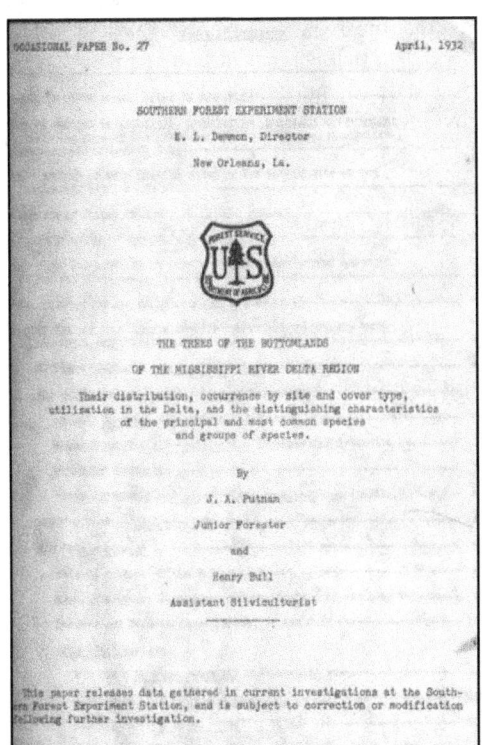

Occasional Paper 27 was the first of the series, although numbered 27 (Putnam and Bull 1932). It set a high standard for this unique publication series in the Southern Forest Experiment Station.

armpit deep on Put. The laborer, who evidently knew the ground well and was pretty sure where the plots lay, said: "You gennelmen come over thisaway. There's a high, dry ridge that'll take us right to the place, and it'll be easier going."

They followed the laborer's lead, and sure enough, the going was easier, as the water was only knee-deep on Gus. They continued a long way, wading up to their knees, and finally Put, who had the shortest legs in the party, said to the laborer: "Where's that high, dry ridge you were going to take us to?"

"Why, Mister," said the laborer, "you're *on* it right now!" and couldn't understand why Gus and Put roared with laughter.

They finally recognized Mattoon's plots, not from the tags on the trees but from Captain Forgey's sense of location, combined with his suspicion regarding certain bumps on the tree trunks. They cut into these bumps and found that each one contained one of Mattoon's brass tags, completely overgrown in the 14 years since the plots had been established. They remeasured the trees and found no appreciable difference in growth between the cypresses with knees and those without. They brought one of the tags into the New Orleans Office, together with the layer of wood that had grown over it. The number cut into the tag was perfectly reproduced with raised, reversed figures on the chip of fine-grained wood.

The thickness of the layer of wood formed over those tags in a mere 14 years should have made us question the general assumption that the growth of cypress was invariably slow. But it didn't; that was a lead, and an important one, that we missed. It remained for Ted Silker's TVA cypress plantations (Iowa State Col. Jour. Sci. 22 (4): 431-448, 1948) to demonstrate some years later, that the species frequently grew quite rapidly. Some years later still, Bill Beaufait (Jour. Forestry 55 (8): 588, 1957) showed that baldcypress characteristically forms great numbers of false rings; it is obvious now that for decades such rings had resulted in gross over-estimates of the ages of cypress trees.

RECOGNITION

What won the Station its widest recognition and acclaim during the second era was yet another new line of research— Ralph M. Lindgren's study of control of sap stain in pine lumber.

Control of Sap Stain

Lindy was hand-picked by Carl Hartley for research in this field, on the strength of personal ability and record and of the subject of his Master's thesis under Stakman at Minnesota; it is difficult or impossible today to single out and appoint a particular desired candidate in this manner. Lindy arrived at the Station in 1928, "attached" to the Bureau of Plant Industry; in 1929, he was listed as an Assistant Pathologist. He had a responsibility far above that of the assistant's (the old P-2) grade, which he carried out, not by authority or by financial or administrative support, but by sheer ability and personality. He was, for many years, of course, one of the Service's notable research workers and research administrators.

During 1928, Lindy treated matched billets of sap pine, and some of hardwood also, with about 250 different chemicals

Captain Forgey led Putnam and Lentz to Mattoon's plots that were established to determine the purpose of cypress knees.

Ralph "Lindy" Lindgren hard at work on his sap stain study in the laboratory he and Paul Siggers shared with Doc Pessin and Phil Wakeley on the sixth floor of the then Sterns Building in New Orleans.

that the literature indicated or that he surmised might control "blue-stain." These billets he arranged in little cribs or piles in the best "blue-stain environment" he could find, namely, underneath stacks of green lumber in the yards of a number of mills at which the sap-stain problem was particularly acute.

As I remember, the summer of 1928 was particularly hot and damp. Anyway, the cramped crawl-spaces beneath the piles were ideal incubators. All the untreated check billets and most of the chemically treated billets were badly stained. Some six of the chemicals, however, showed good promise of controlling the blue-stain fungi. One of these six was ethyl mercury chloride.

In 1929, Lindy reported his preliminary results to the industry. Apparently, his first published article was in Southern Lumberman 136 (1763): 60-62, 1929, but almost surely typescript reports went in advance to cooperating companies and perhaps to one or more trade associations. A second published report appeared in Southern Lumberman 139 (1779): 62, 64, 1930, and in other outlets.

By prodigious feats of persuasion and oratory following his first reports, Lindy got five companies in Florida, Alabama, Mississippi and Louisiana to try his six most promising chemicals on carload lots of green lumber.

This was a serious undertaking. If the chemicals failed to work in this pilot-plant test as they had in the exploratory trials, sap-stain would greatly reduce the value of the treated lumber. The untreated carload lots of fresh lumber required as checks would almost surely be degraded by stain; this would involve a financial loss that could be avoided by kiln-drying—and the country was in the throes of a depression. The chemical treatments, or so it was thought then, required installation of heated dipping troughs, with special conveyers to bring in and immerse the boards; this entailed a cash outlay. And, of course, the experiment meant extra work for yard foremen,

who wouldn't like it and would have to be bullied into doing their part.

Despite these obstacles, Lindy got the support he needed. For 2 or 3 weeks in the spring of 1930, he ran himself ragged, driving from mill to mill to supervise the preparation of the six test solutions and the running of the green lumber through the improvised dipping vats. Finally, about the middle of May, as I recall, all the treated stacks and untreated checks were in place at all the cooperating mills and Lindy could draw a long breath again.

Then there occurred one of those things that don't make good movies but that try the souls of research workers as much as the dangers and uncertainties of any cowboy or explorer whose adventures were ever filmed. We had a drought.

From the time the stacks of lumber were put up until the end of June, humidities were unprecedentedly low and there was little, if any, rain at any of the cooperating mills. Treated and untreated lumber alike dried out extremely fast and even the untreated checks remained as bright and free from stain as though run through the kiln immediately after leaving the saw. Lindy was in despair. Despite his ability and drive, he was still young. He had compromised his Bureau as well as himself by getting the mill men to invest so much money in a large-scale test that was showing absolutely no results. The weeks went by, and finally on a holiday, (he was a bachelor, as he still is, and had no holiday family obligations), he went to the office and poured out his woes by mail to Carl Hartley in Washington.

About the eighth of July, Lindy edged into my office with a self-conscious snicker to show me Hartley's reply. It was a single sentence, though rather a long one. I assume I remember the date correctly and I am confident that I quote the letter verbatim, even after all these years. I should be able to; it has tided me over many a difficult situation since, even

Air-drying freshly cut lumber under warm, humid conditions resulted in the development of blue-stain and diminished market value.

the loss of 8 years' experimental planting at Alexandria to fire and hogs during World War II. It read:

> Dear Lindy:
> The only reply I have to your lugubrious 7-page letter of July 4, is the somewhat exotic one that Metcalf made to me when I voiced a similar complaint about a damping-off study at the Monument Nursery: 'Allah be praised! Continue!'

This letter bucked Lindy up immensely.

A few days later a rainy period set in. The untreated check billets, like the check and the ineffectively treated test billets in the preliminary trials, turned practically black with sap stain. The lumber treated with some of the more promising chemicals stained pretty badly also. But the number treated with ethyl mercury chloride remained consistently bright at all the cooperating mills.

Lindy reported the results factually and ungrammatically in several trade journals. Apparently though, word-of-mouth reports outstripped and overshadowed publication. Certainly industry—both lumber and chemical—was keenly interested.

In 1931, Lindy demonstrated that ethyl mercury chloride could be applied effectively at air temperature; this obviated the need for the specially heated dipping vats. A few disquieting failures of the dip were definitely traced to belated or improper application of the chemical, or to blue-stain infection in logs held too long or under adverse conditions before sawing. Ethyl mercury chloride appeared on the market under the trade name of Lignasan, which is still the standard dip for controlling blue-stain. The Station's Annual Report

Lindgren served as director of the Station's Division of Plant Pathology until 1952 when he moved to the Forest Products Lab in Madison, WS.

for 1931 records the use of Lignasan at more than 100 mills and by the following year, it was being used at 200 pine and hardwood mills in this country and was rapidly coming into use abroad.

To this one research accomplishment, I feel more than to any other single activity or achievement, the Station owed its first general and unqualified recognition and support. From the time that chemical control of sap stain became common practice, it was a distinction simply to be on the Station staff.

The Southern Forest Survey

Meanwhile another new venture of the Station, destined to confirm and extend the reputation established by the sap-stain control project, was getting under way. This was the Southern Forest Survey part of the nationwide timber survey, by the Forest Service, that had been authorized and prescribed by the McNary-McSweeney Act. Officially and ostensibly, it began January 1, 1931. Actually the foundation—recruitment of personnel and formulation of plans—was begun in 1930. Doubtless the details of this foundation could be constructed from documents still extant in New Orleans; Wheeler and Lehrbas (both retired now) could trace them more easily than I. Certainly Lentz returned to the Station, on permanent appointment, early in 1930, to guide the initial steps, and he, Lehrbas (Assistant Forest Economist in late 1930 or early 1931), Cruikshank (Junior Forester, 1930), Wheeler (Junior Forester in late 1930 or early 1931), Bob Winters, (Assistant Silviculturist, 1930) and I think Putnam (Junior Forester, 1931) in the hardwood phases, played important roles in planning and in early fieldwork. (Roy Chapman, both before his detail to the Washington Office in 1931 and after his return in 1934, contributed unofficially but nonetheless effectively to Survey sampling techniques and analyses; even in 1931, he probably was the ablest statistician at the Station.) In 1932, Cap Eldredge joined the staff as Principal Forest Economist to direct the Survey; later, The Survey and Financial Aspects of Timber Growing were merged into the late Division of Forest Economics Research, Cap became Division Chief, a position he held till his retirement in 1944.

Though a man of vision and at once sagacious and intensely practical, Cap was not a trained economist and he was by no means a statistician. I remember lunching one day in Morrison's cafeteria at The Masonic Temple on St. Charles Street with him, Bob Winters and Phil Wheeler, after he had spent a long, hard morning with Bob and Phil on some of the more technical statistical problems of the survey.

Cap remarked that he was thinking of breaking his leg.

It would hurt, of course, but after all, he was a man and could bear the pain and it wouldn't last long. After the worst pain was over, ladies would bring him calves-foot jelly; he didn't care especially for calve-foot jelly, but he'd appreciate the attention.

About the end of the third day, he'd cease to be a nine-days' wonder and people would leave him alone and he would have time for serious study. Statistics, for example. (At this point, Bob and Phil suddenly realized Cap was getting back at them for the morning's technicalities.)

Yes, statistics. For example, he had always wanted to make a statistical study of wife-beaters!

For a long time now he had had a theory—or more correctly, a hypothesis—that if you took a group of men who were scrupulously honest in business affairs and didn't drink or smoke or swear and were deacons in the church, you would find a significantly higher percentage of them, than of the general population, were wife-beaters. After all, he said, a man has to have *some* relaxation!

Of course, he added as a parting shot after the laughter had died down, you'd have to exclude from the sample the men who had a *right* to beat their wives.

Facetious? Yes. But the Survey itself was a serious undertaking carried out ably and vigorously. I do not think that the Southern Station's handling of its share of it was second to any in our country. Don't make the mistake of deprecating the work in the South on the count of "easy topography!" The flatwoods and the Delta are mighty hot in summer. We used to have a photo of a

Phil Wheeler (right) joined the Station in 1931 and served as the Coast Guard's Captain of the Port New Orleans during World War II. He was given the USDA Superior Service Award in 1962 for his contributions to improving forest survey techniques. Dr. R.S. Campbell (left), a botanist, was one of the founders of the Society of Range Management.

Mississippi bottomland crew, their heads just showing above, or through, an almost impenetrable tangle of poison ivy. According to Winters, the swamps near Grand Lake and Morgan City were traversed generally on hands and knees. And one man on the crew surveying the Burris Dam watershed—some man I had never met—was injured in a fall in a rocky gorge and later died of his injury. We could not recompense his widow financially because nobody had recorded the fall in his official diary.

I have not attempted to trace the first pressagentings of the Survey in speeches and addresses, in the trade journals, in Service official-organs and in the Station's Annual Reports. Eldredge's "The Southern Forest Survey" was issued under date of June 1, 1934 as Occasional Paper 31, to be followed in August 1934 by Occasional Paper 34, "The proportion of diameter classes in the longleaf-slash pine stands of southeast Georgia" and in October 1934 by Occasional Paper 36, "Classification of working turpentine cups in south Georgia by year of working and turpentine history of worked trees." These three Occasional Papers were later relisted as Forest Survey Releases 1, 2 and 3 and were followed, still in 1934, by Forest Survey Release No. 4 (so labelled), "Gum naval stores production, producing acreage and number of working cups in Forest Survey Unit #1, Georgia."

Release No.1 (Occasional Paper 31) was little more than a promissory note. "It is estimated that more than half a million tabulating machine cards will be required," and, in the caption of a pretty picture, "The published reports...will show the volume of virgin longleaf pine in the South." It did, however, record 19 3-man crews at work and 39,380,000 acres surveyed between January 1, 1931 and June 1, 1934.

Releases 2 and 3 (Occasional Papers 34 and 36) and Release No. 4 did report findings, but only the simplest and easiest to get cut of the cards. Information on diameter distributions, turpentine-cup classifications, and gum production and producing acreage was not released because of urgent demand for it during the Depression, but because it could be published promptly and would make a showing of Station and particularly of Survey publication. I mean nothing derogatory by this statement. The figures were as valid as the techniques then developed would permit and it was sound strategy to publish them.

Then, next to the last release of 1934, came No. 5, "Advance information on the supply of pulpwood in Survey Unit #1, Georgia." This was what industry and a host of others wanted. It was in great demand and widely quoted. Further releases were eagerly expected. The Survey's reputation was made and that of the Station greatly enhanced. An agency that could lick the blue-stain problem for the lumbermen and then pin-point the raw material on which the pulp and paper industry depended for its very existence must amount to something after all.

By the end of 1942, the first year of World War II, the Southern Survey had gridironed the States from South Carolina and part of Tennessee south and west to the western boundaries of the southern pines and had issued 53 releases, which in turn had been reworked into formal State reports issued from the Government Printing Office. This was a tremendous and worthwhile job. The territory was resurveyed by the Southeastern and Southern Stations beginning in 1946 and the third Survey is now well on its way to completion. Perhaps it's rather routine now. Current data on the forest resource, once original and novel luxuries, have become virtual necessaries, like automobiles and flush toilets that our present culture can't do without. And the thrill, to hear the Survey staff talk, has largely gone out of the statistical techniques of sampling, out of mensurational techniques (even out of photogrammetry) and out of the practical problems of getting to and getting back from the plots in the woods. If the Survey still has a link with original research, I imagine it may be in connection with basic economic theory. But bringing the survey to this routine pass had much to do with the Station's coming of age.

Erosion and Flood Control Research

Another new line of work started during this era was flood and erosion control by means of forest cover. In a sense, this was an outgrowth of the 1927 flood study. At the time of that study and for some time after we began our own erosion control experiments in the South, we were unaware of Lowdermilk's work on the effect of litter and humus in maintaining infiltration rate by keeping soil pores unsealed. Lowdermilk may not even have established his first impact-absorption and porosity-maintenance experiments when our erosion-control program was undertaken.

The hero of our erosion-control program was H.G. Meginnis.

In October 1929, not long after Mac's appointment as Junior Forester and Don Sinclair's appointment as Assistant Forest Ecologist, Mac, Don and I toured the Mississippi bluff country from Natchez south to Woodville, looking for horrible examples of erosion to control. Although we discovered at Woodville a bathtub long enough to accommodate even Don's long frame, (so long in fact, that we wondered how it had been ferried around the bends of the Mississippi River!), the trip was disappointing. The bluffs, despite their loessal composition, just weren't eroding enough to get excited about.

That same year or early the next, Don, Mac and I think Gus Lentz (who worked briefly on erosion control between his Survey assignment and his transfer to the TVA in 1933) discovered Lafayette and Marshall counties in northern Mississippi, where loess less deep than that in the bluffs was underlain by alternate strata of permeable sand and impermeable clay. Here erosion was a problem beyond any doubt. Gullies had eaten entire farms away, had severed some country roads and were threatening some main highways; the sediment from the gullies was burying rich farmland in the Yazoo bottoms so deeply in sterile sand that they could never grow crops again.

The boys illegally cut a window in the side of a panel truck so they could see out both sides (this made the truck a "Passenger Car" in contravention of the limitation on the number of passenger vehicles the Station might operate), and by driving practically all the roads in the two counties, made a crop-meter survey of conditions. This survey showed nearly 35 percent of the two counties in active gullies, from a foot or two to 80 or 100 feet deep. The percentage seemed unbelievably high and was generally attributed to biased sampling, arising from

Soil erosion resulting from the removal of forest stands for agriculture was a major problem in portions of the South. North Mississippi was particularly susceptible to erosion and Meginnis conducted much of his research in this area. In the late 1940s, the Yazoo-Tallahatchie Flood Prevention Project was established to apply the research techniques developed by Meginnis' research (Williston 1988).

the fact that the roads driven over with the crop-meter were practically all on the ridges. Nevertheless, the Southern Forest Survey, run independently of roads, later confirmed the figure almost exactly and subsequent aerial photographs made it even larger. So far as Lafayette and Marshall counties were concerned, we were forced to conclude that the land of the free and the home of the brave was literally going down the drain.

Mac established headquarters at Holly Springs, Mississippi— this was some years before the purchase of the Holly Springs National Forest—made some sort of arrangements for experimental use of an old, badly gullied field and went to work. He worked largely single-handed at first, with occasional visits of guidance, advice and assistance from Station overhead or fellow workers. Ivy Olsen took his place in the latter part of 1933 to release him for attendance at some meeting; I am not sure that the Meginnises' first baby was not born while Ivy was there in Mac's place. Tenyo Maki's first service at the Southern Station was as Mac's Temporary Field Assistant. For the most part, however, Mac worked alone or with temporary local labor.

His research, which was both basic and applied, was exemplary. He devised small plots, surrounded by wide strips of galvanized iron with the lower edges sunk into the ground, whereby he obtained startling data on erosion and run-off on several soil types on several degrees of slope, on bare surfaces, and under both grass and tree cover. Misled by notions then current, he planted a lot of black locust, which proved out of place in that setting, but he also planted a lot of pine, which ultimately revolutionized erosion-control practice in the South. In his work with locust, he developed and published a technique for scarifying the seed with sulfuric acid to promote germination; this has since proved widely useful in places where black locust is worth growing, and has also been used with seed of other species. I visited Mac's studies at Holly Springs in the spring of 1933, enroute north with my family on leave, by car, and found his program, experimental design and experimental techniques stimulating to a degree.

Mac's most striking experiment, at least to me, was the "calibration" of two pairs of small plots in terms of run-off and erosion in and after rainstorms of varying intensity. All four plots were close together and basically similar in soil and slope, but two were in a blackjack oak thicket and two were on the bare soil of an old field.

Mac calibrated all four plots in enough storms to show conclusively that the two bare plots were not only closely similar one to the other in run-off and soil-loss, but were also subject to much more run-off and to many-fold the soil loss of the two plots in the oak thicket.

Then he reversed covers on the two pairs. He removed all the litter and unincorporated organic matter from each of the plots in the thicket, placed this material on the corresponding bare plots in the abandoned field and fastened it there with coarse chicken wire. As additional leaves fell on the oak plots, he transferred them to the corresponding old-field plots, keeping the surface of the soil in the oak plots bare.

Under Meginnis' direction, Junior Forester "Ivy" Olsen and Temp. Field Asst. Tenyo Ewald Maki, are planting in a gully control project at Holly Springs, MS, in 1932.

The next few rainstorms told the story. Run-off from the old field plots, now protected by litter, was greatly reduced and erosion practically ceased. Run-off and erosion from the now bare plots under the oaks approached very closely that originally found on the old-field plots. Publication of the data created quite a stir. They were widely quoted and greatly influenced subsequent land-use planning and policy decisions.

All this time, Mac was still only a Junior Forester and a down-trodden one at that. To provide a laboratory in which to treat seed, measure seedlings and weigh the soil samples from his experimental plots, he purchased, with official approval and official funds, a small abandoned chicken house; I believe it cost $5 delivered at the gully in which he had made arrangements to work. The chicken house turned out to be swarming with chicken lice. These he eliminated, or at least materially reduced, with an insecticidal spray. He paid some seventy-five cents for the spray and included the item in his next expense account. The item was disallowed by the General Accounting Office and continued to be disallowed despite all efforts on the part of the Station, on the grounds that getting rid of the distracting lice was for the personal benefit of the employee, not for the benefit of the Government. Contrast this with the perquisites enjoyed by astronauts today!

Shortly thereafter though, justice was done. The Soil Erosion Service—now the Soil Conservation Service—was formed. Universities leaped for the bandwagon. Mac received numerous offers of jobs in other bureaus and in universities. He was almost the only erosion-control specialist the Service had and the only one with experience and research accomplishments in the Lower South. The Service had to hold him to compete, and to hold him, it reallocated him, at one jump from Junior Forester P-1 to full Silviculturist P-4. This unprecedented promotion could not have befallen a nicer

H.G. Meginnis' research in erosion control has been applied across the nation on severely eroded sites.

fellow or one less likely to presume upon it.

The second era saw the beginning of studies of the economics of timber growing, and also of forest taxation studies, as distinct from the Forest Survey's assessment of the forest resource. (At first, while Dr. Ziegler was at the Station, Survey and Economics were separate Divisions; ultimately, they were merged under Eldredge.)

Of the earlier economics studies, such as that of "roofers" (which proved to be the principal product) in Alcorn County, Mississippi, I can say very little. The findings, although reported with a sprightly air at the time, have been lost in obscurity. Their release apparently had little effect. The same seems to be true of any and all forest taxation studies, those made of late years by the present Economics staff as well as the original ones made by Ron Craig. I have formed the perhaps hazy and inexact impression that forest taxation in the South lies in the sphere of politics rather than of forest economics and that nothing the Station has been able to find out about it can reasonably be expected to affect it.

Crossett

The big thing, other than the Southern Forest Survey, that grew out of the economics studies was the entity known successively as the Crossett Experimental Forest, Crossett Research Center, Crossett Forest Management Project and today, Crossett Timber Management Project. Different names, same entity.

More or less coincident with his leaving the Crossett Company to join the Station staff in 1932, Wackerman played a considerable part in arranging the cooperation between the Company and the Forest Service, including the donation of the Crossett Experimental Forest to the Service—that is, to the Station—by the Company. I never knew the details of his contribution and have forgotten most of those concerning the cooperative agreement; the latter certainly are still available, however, in the Station's stuffier archives.

The original Crossett Experimental Forest established under the cooperative agreement included, according to the 1935 Annual Report, either 1,628 or 1,680 acres. Most of

it was relatively well stocked second-growth loblolly-(and some shortleaf)-hardwood type. As it lay less than 12 miles on a main highway, from a combined paper mill and pineand hardwood sawmill, with a destructive-distillation plant attached, it was an ideal setup for intensive management through close utilization.

Under the cooperative agreement, we were to return to the Company within the next 20 years, the equivalent of the stand present on the Forest when it was placed under management. This stand was estimated in September 1934 as 8 million feet (gross scale, International log rule) of sawtimber, 8,700 cords of pulpwood and 6,600 cords of chemical wood. Russ Reynolds, who initiated management and has maintained it ever since, seemed entirely happy with this contract and I never heard Demmon or anyone from Washington express concern over it. The rank and file of silviculturists on the staff, however, particularly Gemmer and I, and I think Wahlenberg also, were very apprehensive about it. We had visions of gross overcutting toward the end of the 20-year period to fulfill the agreement. We needn't have worried. Under Russ' skillful treatment, the full tally of wood was delivered within the prescribed time, leaving the Forest better stocked than when we first took it over. Such is the productive capacity of southern pine on good sites and in good hands.

Russ Reynolds skill in managing the Crossett Experimental Forest was widely recognized and the forest became a showcase for good forest management.

I for one was even more worried about the objectives of the research on the Forest and about the experimental treatments applied than I was about the danger of overcutting. (I spoke out about this once at an "open" meeting at Crossett, at which non-Service personnel, including H.H. Chapman, were present in a way that led even the mild and charitable Wahlenberg to reprimand me for indecorum.) The Forest was organized in the heyday of "selective cutting," that system of management vociferously distinguished from the "single-tree selection system of silviculture" but otherwise amorphous except that it involved a multiplicity of age (or was it size?) classes. The Forest was deliberately and avowedly set up to "demonstrate" the virtues of such selective cutting. Voluminous records were kept on initial and subsequent stocking, growth, yields, costs, returns and estimate values on the stump and at the roadside, but the only experimental treatments applied to the 40-acre compartments into which most of the Forest (1,003 acres) was divided were cutting cycles of different lengths—3, 6 and 9 years, as I recall. Although these cycles were replicated, there was no even-aged management check.

Not that loblolly pine cannot be grown, and profitably, in many age classes on each 40 acres. It can be; Russ Reynolds has done it for 30 years, as his meticulous records and the immense present value of the original Crossett Experimental Forest attest. But this unabashed move to "demonstrate" the worth of a current fad and particularly the failure to match many-aged management with the most obvious check, namely, even-aged management, seemed to me a regression to the days when the McNeill experiment was laid out, with no periodic burning treatment included, to "demonstrate" the evils of any fire whatever in the longleaf pine type.

It seems to me noteworthy in this connection that the Crossett Company, originally committed to many-aged

management, was finally forced by brush-invasion and reproduction troubles to go over to even-aged management; that shortly after World War II the Station felt impelled to lease an additional 2,000 acres from the Crossett Company and place it under even-aged management as a belated check on the many-aged compartments of the original tract; that even-aged management is practically universal on the vast pulpwood-industry ownership in the southern pine types; and that, effective in 1961, the shortleaf pine on the Ouachita National Forest was at long last ordered converted to even-aged management. Perhaps the Ouachita would have been converted sooner, if at Crossett, we had from the start made a direct comparison between the two systems.

Despite what I consider its long run with only half its cylinders firing—and the poorer half at that!—there is no denying the immense impetus that the Crossett Experimental Forest, under Russ Reynolds' direction, has given both to the Station and to technical forestry throughout the South. The data it has yielded on many-aged management, even without the obvious check, are uniquely valuable. A multitude of collateral studies, both silvicultural and economic, have been a gold-mine of information; witness the literally hundreds of citations of articles by Reynolds and his Crossett colleagues in Wahlenberg's "Loblolly Pine." The Crossett Project's contribution to forest tree improvement are not to be lightly brushed aside and will grow in value as the trees in its hybrid-, progeny- and provenance-test plantations grow tall.

As a demonstration area, the Crossett Experimental Forest has had no peer in the Station territory. Its visitors number thousands every year and have included foresters from every quarter of the globe. "Farm Forty Day" each year draws crowds of professional foresters, woodland managers and practical owners of small tracts, to see the annual cut from

Reynolds interacting with 4-H students at one of his "Farm Forty Days" on the Crossett Experimental Forest.

two areas of roughly 40 acres each, one originally "poor" and the other "good." Over the past quarter, only Russ has, with consummate skill, converted the poor forty to as highly productive a stand as the good one, with a fair to substantial profit from each stand each year.

Truly, the Crossett Experimental Forest, ranks high among the monuments of both expansion and recognition that had their start in the Second Era.

Forest Pathologist Paul Siggers

I have mentioned the instrumentality of the 1928 fire at Bogalusa in getting Paul Siggers detailed to the Station. In his quiet manner, Paul Siggers started something fully as important as the Crossett Experimental Forest, for he was, so far as I am aware, the pioneer in carrying research on southern forest tree diseases beyond the stage of mycological taxonomy. Certainly his studies of brown spot during the Era of Expansion and Recognition and of fusiform rust during the era that followed, had far-reaching effects on forest practice and on long-range plans for both forest research and extensive forest management. Since 1951, they have had a considerable impact on forest genetics. The lines of work that he initiated proliferated during Civilian Conservation Corps days into Lamb's and Sleeth's studies of fusiform rust and other diseases in forest nurseries. Siggers did the initial work on littleleaf disease and, if I remember correctly, gave that disease its official common name. His undertakings survived World War II. Directly or indirectly, they gave rise to Berch Henry's work on root rot at the Ashe Nursery, to W.A. Campbell's and Bratislav Zak's work on littleleaf, to Dick Toole's studies of bottom-land hardwood diseases and to Fred Jewell's breeding for rust resistance. A thread of continuity runs through all of these and Verrall till June 1964, our Forest Disease Division Chief, started his southern career under Siggers at Bogalusa, on the earlier brown spot studies.

I deliberately used the adjective *quiet* in re-introducing Paul Siggers into this narrative. Although a gregarious, cordial, widely congenial man, he tended to speak only at long intervals and briefly then. A night on which I shared a room with him in the old Pine Tree Inn at Bogalusa was typical.

The window and screen in the room were such that unless left just so, mosquitoes got in. When we returned from the field at supper time, we found that the maid had adjusted the window otherwise and that the mosquitoes had taken over.

After supper we went out to a drug store and I bought a Saturday Evening Post. When we returned to our room, I joined Paul in killing the less nimble mosquitoes. Then I settled down to read.

Not so Paul. He wet a towel and went after the pests in earnest. I made several spritely comments. Paul smiled, said nothing and continued to chase mosquitoes. He knocked dust off the picture molding onto my pillow, gave me his pillow in exchange and turned the soiled pillowcase inside out for his own use. Each mosquito that he killed, he added silently to a row on the wash basin. Finally, after I had read two long stories, he set the table on his bed, still without a word, mounted it precariously to kill the last mosquito in the room, and added the corpse to his collection on the washbowl. Then, still silently, he put the room to rights and washed his hands. Finally he counted his collection of corpses, turned to me with the sweetest smile a man ever smiled, and said: "I don't like mosquitoes."

The Pine Tree Inn in Bogalusa was built in 1907 by the Great Southern Lumber Company to house business associates and visitors (Goodyear 1950).

An able scientist with work habits like that can do an impressive amount of research over the years. It has taken many men, with highly specialized training, new techniques and equipment and financing such as Paul may have dreamed of but never had (and characteristically never mentioned!) to go much beyond his findings. This is the more remarkable in that he had no statistical background and, short of man-power as he was, handicapped himself further by incorporating grossly extravagant margins of safety in the numbers of measurements he took and by failing to analyze them exhaustively. He must, however, have been fertile in hypotheses (though he spoke sparingly of them also), and the strength of his research lay in testing each hypothesis regarding brown spot, rust or any other disease or influence, in several to many completely independent studies. In effect, he sampled more comprehensively and more completely at random and replicated more extensively at the level at which replication really counted, than more statistically expert pathologists might have done.

Paul published rather sparingly—only some 30 articles and notes, many of them quite short—in his 20-odd years at the Station. I think procedure within the Bureau that assigned him to the Station, may have had some part in limiting his output. He did, however, write an immense number of office reports and special technical memoranda. I have had occasion to abstract literally scores of them in preparing reports and publications of my own, and it is in the light of this familiarity with his work that I rank Paul Siggers as one of the clearest and most precise technical writers I have ever known.

The Occasional Papers

No record of the Station's expansion and recognition between 1928 and 1933 would be complete without mention of the series of Occasional Papers initiated at the very end of that period. The series was outlawed at the end of 1962. Its genesis, in retrospect, was laughable. Some of its individual components were hardly worth mimeograph paper on which these releases at first appeared. In the event of a fire, however, I probably would save my complete file of the papers in preference to my annotated file of the *Journal of Forestry* from 1922 to date. Certainly the *Papers* are the finer collector's item.

The way the series started was this.

Annually or thereabouts, during the early Thirties, we issued lists of publications by the Station staff. The term "publication" was used in the broadest sense; in addition to government bulletins and reprints from professional journals, it included mimeographed texts of the Director's trade-association speeches and even Pessin's 1-page, letter-size popular chart showing "How a Tree Grows." In each annual list, the items still available on request, were marked with asterisks.

The list issued in late 1932 or early 1933 included 27 items so marked. They varied from the 1-page chart just mentioned

to Putnam and Bull's 210-page mimeographed monograph, "The trees of the bottomlands of the Mississippi River Delta Region", which certainly was one of the two or three best research publications of the Station up to that time, and perhaps of all time.

With this list at hand, Director Demmon conceived the idea of thenceforth numbering consecutively all mimeographed releases from the Station. (I don't recall whether this was entirely on his own initiative or in part an outgrowth of the easy, informal conferences we then used to hold regarding Station affairs.) Numbering them in a named series would, he thought, tie them together and emphasize their connection with the Station and would make them easier to cite.

The scheme had further merits.

The caption "Occasional Paper" was distinctive. I don't recall that any other Station or agency ever used it and certainly it was far superior to the stuttering designation, "Blank Station *Station Paper*" adopted in some other quarters—though I am not sure Demmon didn't invent that one too!

The caption presaged the appearance of papers at irregular intervals, as data worth releasing became available. There was no implied commitment to a publication deadline like that of an annual report or of a monthly professional journal. Neither was there a stated limitation on space, as in the regular number of pages per month commonly set on a journal. Length, style and contents could be varied to fit the results to be reported. This flexibility has been a great asset to the Station. In 1951, it even made possible the release (in three volumes, totaling 579 pages) of 800 copies of my own "Planting the southern pines" in the form in which it was submitted to Washington for Government Printing Office publication—a move which effactually precluded Washington Office alterations of the contents.

Most important of all, release could be timely. Review outside the Station, and in particular by the Washington Office, was omitted and rapidity of processing and proofing was limited only by our own energy and ability. We safeguarded ourselves, in the use of these shortcuts, by stating on the front cover of each Occasional Paper that: "This series of publications releases data gathered in connection with investigations being carried out at the Southern Station. The information contained in them is subject to correction or amplification following further investigation." Very rarely indeed, however, did we have to issue a correction to a paper and I do not recall that we ever retracted a conclusion published in the series. True, some findings became passé as time went on, but this phenomenon is of general occurrence. Some papers were sound enough and in enough demand to require verbatim reissue.

Although it has been fashionable to deprecate the Occasional Papers and although some individual papers have in fact been trivial, the series was soundly conceived to meet a real need. Chronologically, the series was a pioneer in this type of Service research release. The crudeness with which the earlier papers were processed reflected only the crudeness and meagerness of all our facilities in those days. The papers, as time went on, became increasingly well written, well edited, well designed and well printed. They have had a world-wide circulation. Many, even of the earlier and more primitive ones, have been widely quoted in textbooks and periodicals. A few have become classics in their particular fields of research.

Why then, have I described the genesis of the series as laughable?

Well, the very first Occasional Paper issued was "Truck Logging of Pine in Mississippi and Louisiana." It was written by Russ Reynolds while he was still a Junior Forester and I doubt whether Russ regards it as one of his more important contributions. The facts it contains "were obtained as a result of visits to a fairly large and representative number of companies doing truck logging in parts of central Mississippi and eastern Louisiana," and are presented largely in descriptive narrative form, though with some tabular material on length of haul, stands logged, volumes per load in wet and dry weather, round trips per day on different types of road and facts as related to all these. The paper notes the increasing replacement of railroad logging by truck logging, stresses the value of trucks in connection with selective logging and concludes with the statement that with proper decking of logs, off the ground and with pole stringers between tiers, there is

little or no danger of blue-stain from the latter part of October to the middle of March.

This opus is a scant ten pages in length, mimeographed, single-spaced without illustrations. It was issued in July 1933. And because we had 27 earlier reprints, charts and mimeographed speeches still available for distribution, as shown by asterisks in the 1932 list of publications, Demmie numbered Reynolds' observations on truck logging Occasional Paper 28!

I know. I know. Putnam and Bull's magnificent "Trees of the bottomlands…exists as Occasional Paper 27, dated April 1932. But that is a back-numbered, back-dated reissue, whether from the original or from retyped mimeograph stencils, I have not taken the time to be certain. The original issue of "Trees of the bottomlands…, that finally came out in 1932, was unnumbered. I have my unnumbered copy too.

Even counting this back-dated and numbered reissue, the Station has released only 168 Occasional Papers in 30 years instead of the 194 indicated by the highest number in the series, at the close of 1962.

Can the designation of our first Occasional Paper as "Number 28" have been the first stirrings of an impulse toward the modern game of "creating an image?"

ORGANIZATION AND ADMINISTRATION

Divisions

During the Era of Expansion and Recognition, a number of events took place that affected the Station's organization and program for many years to come. One of the more obvious of these was the grouping of the staff into separate Divisions.

Originally, all the work of the Station in protection, management, mensuration, naval stores and forestation, (the "Cinderella project") was under one Division, that of Silvical Research. Silvical Research was later renamed Forest Management Research, and this in turn in 1964, became Timber Management Research.

About 1929 or 1930, separate Divisions of Forest Economics and Forest Survey were set up. (An hour or two of intensive library research might give me the exact date, the authority and so on but for present purposes, I am content to let the approximation stand.) Ziegler was the first Division Chief in Charge of Economics and was succeeded by Bond. Lentz began the organization of Forest Survey, but to the best of my recollection, Eldredge was the first formally appointed Division Chief in charge. Subsequently, as I have already mentioned, Survey and Economics were combined in one Division under Eldredge. At long and irregular intervals,

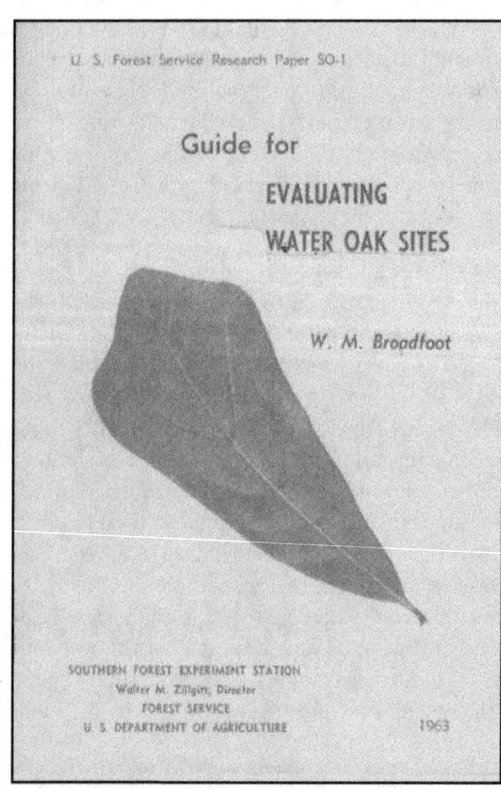

Research Paper SO-1 began the new series that replaced the Occasional Papers when Forest Service Research was reorganized in 1964.

other Divisions—Forest Influences, Range Research, Disease, Insects, Forest Utilization Service—were added and variously renamed and combined. It's a long and complex story, not to be gone into here. The point is that the separate Divisions that, until the sweeping reorganization of 1964, functioned and were the essential framework of the Station, first took form about 1930.

When the members of the staff were first assigned to separate Divisions, Demmon remained "ex officio" Division Chief of Silvical Research (Protection, Management, etc.) and Project or Subproject leader in charge of Fire Protection. Silvical Research was at that time far and away the most important Division and Fire Protection had the highest priority in it and heading up these lines of work was Demmon's perogative as Director. His duties as Director of an expanding organization left him little time, however, for detailed supervision of his own Division or for personal research in his own Project. Furthermore, there were times when he quieted, at the expense of Silvics, the insistent demands of Economics and Survey for facilities and funds. While we were in the Union Building (now the Richards Center) at Baronne and Gravier, for example, Silvics paid the rent not only on its own office space but also on the more commodious space allotted to Eldredge's Survey. It did, that is, until Les Harper was appointed Division Chief of Silvics, under Demmon, and co-equal with Division Chiefs Bond and Eldredge. Then things changed, but that episode occurred in the next era.

Executive Assistant

During the first 8 years of the Station's existence, Vera Spuhler, as Head Clerk, handled all the details of the Station's accounts and all such related matters as payroll, property and supplies. Then, in late 1928 or early 1929, we acquired a "Junior Administrative Assistant," with the title of Executive Assistant, to take over with a clerk and ultimately several clerks of his own, these phases of the Station's work. This Executive Assistant, John A. Lubbe, was in a sense the pollen which fertilized the seed from which germinated our present thriving Division of Station Management. The pedigree is preserved in the records for all to read.

Jack Lubbe came to us after 5 years as a District Ranger—one of the old breed of rangers, without professional training— on the Nebraska National Forest. He was a great, strapping fellow, very like heavyweight champion Jack Dempsey in appearance but much handsomer. A capable man with a forceful personality, he always seemed to me the typical top sergeant of song and story, complete even to rough practical jokes and unrepeatable anecdotes, but not as if it were commissioned. He certainly got things done but his approach to his work was wholly empirical and he was arbitrary to a degree.

Jack had an avowed eye for figures; indeed, the other men on the staff were firmly convinced that he selected his own clerks (with one notable exception) on the basis of d.b.h. His stock

E.L. Demmon was Director of the Southern Station during a period of remarkable growth and productivity—1927 to 1944.

reply when you needed manpower or equipment for research was: "I am not in favor of getting that right now"—a stand which did, to be sure, save writing out purchase orders and time slips. He refused for 9 years to act on either the quarterly inventories of property at Bogalusa that was required of me or on the accompanying Forms 858 (property lost, stolen or damaged), then tried to straighten out the resulting mess by holding the cost of a compound microscope out of my salary. (He lost out on that one; I had recorded the lens numbers and was able to prove Lubbe had given and charged the instrument to another man in my absence, after originally charging it to me.) When we tried to hire a day laborer for 75 cents to load a pick-up truck with coal for the furnace in the Harrison Experimental Forest greenhouse, Jack said: "No. Let Red Watkins (the Station Biologist) do it." We have to pay his salary anyway, so his time isn't worth anything." This attitude, as the part of the man who held the purse strings and who interpreted regulations for the Station, contributed little to the morale of young professional men.

For one thing, however, I give Jack Lubbe unstinted credit. This was his performance as Personnel Officer, a special function that Demmon added to his other assignments in the latter Thirties. Jack threw himself energetically into a study of the regulations affecting promotions and personnel actions and of individual case histories. He must have begun it before the passage of the Meade-Ramspeck Act (the date of which I do not recall), when it was discouragingly easy for a good but undramatic clerk or scientist to get stuck for years at one step within grade. "Ivy" Olsen, for example, an exceptionally able man, remained at Junior Forester entrance salary in this way for 7 years, simply because his assignments gave him no opportunity to publish.

Lubbe unearthed and corrected several injustices of this sort among both men and girls.

Later, when a personnel action was instituted against Doc Pessin on the trumped up grounds that his publication record was unsatisfactory, Lubbe risked the displeasure of one or more superiors by showing that Doc was one of the Station's most prolific authors and that demand for one of his papers in particular had set an all-time record. When it was then re-charged that Doc's publications were "not up to Departmental standards," Lubbe challenged Station overhead to produce the standards. As no such standards had ever been reduced to writing, overhead was unable to supply a copy and the intended action against Doc fell through. In this affair, Lubbe taught the Station a wholesome and needed lesson.

The McNeill Tract

Toward the end of the Era of Expansion and Recognition, we solved an immediate and apparently serious problem in a way that saddled us with a worse problem for many years to come. The immediate problem was saving our big study at McNeill, Mississippi, of the effects of fire and grazing on longleaf pine reproduction. Experimental treatments had begun in 1923. In late 1929 or early 1930, Mr. Tate, from whom we leased the area, decided to sell the lands, the sooner the better. We had an almost idolatrous veneration for 5-year re-examination cycles in any studies. In the case of the McNeill study, we were confident that a full decade of treatment and re-examinations would give us definitive results. And we badly wanted such results for use in our then current controversy with H.H. Chapman, of the Yale School of Forestry, regarding the role of fire in the longleaf pine type. Therefore, we countered Tate's desire to sell by making a strenuous and ultimately successful effort to have the

National Forest Reservation Commission purchase the leased section and most of an adjacent section for permanent use as an experimental area.

The rest of the story extends clear through to the present era.

Briefly, the National Forest Reservation Commission objected to the purchase, on the grounds that the tract was too far from other National Forest holdings for efficient administration and second, that the price was too high. But it finally bought the land.

The negotiations saved us from having to abandon the McNeill study before its tenth year. In fact, they dragged on till after the study, the results of which proved rather disappointing after all, had been completed. Indeed, they dragged on until after F.D. Roosevelt's "New Deal" emergency purchases had brought the Biloxi Ranger District into being and we had laid out the much larger, more conveniently situated Harrison Experimental Forest in a more representative example of the longleaf-slash type.

With the Harrison Experimental Forest practically assured, we tried to halt acquisition of the McNeill Tract. But we couldn't; the procedure we had invoked was too ponderous to stop. The purchase went through and we had on our hands, in addition to the Harrison, more than a thousand acres of highly productive forest land in Pearl River County, miles from our main work and from any National Forest unit and highly vulnerable to fire, hogs and timber trespass.

We then made matters worse by devoting the newly purchased area to a "compartment study" of the type fashionable and extravagantly admired in the Thirties. Such studies have since proved a generally inefficient means of silvicultural research and have fallen into corresponding disrepute. Their cost in labor, professional manpower, material (heavy equipment, roadbuilding, fire suppression, fencing against hogs) and regulatory wrangling, is high. They yield immense quantities of highly variable data, which in turn cost much professional and clerical salary to reduce. Yet the yield in either revolutionary or precise research results is, as a rule, small.

Prof. H.H. Chapman's research established the value of fire in longleaf pine management.

Phil Wakeley standing beside the sign identifying the McNeil Tract.

It seems to me that compartment studies involve an insidious indirect cost in addition to the direct financial outlay. The man in charge of such a study, unless he is both inspired and phenomenally lucky, suffers a severe professional handicap.

The cost of maintaining his compartment study is disproportionally high; everybody knows this and subconsciously associates the cost with the man. There are exasperating complications in connection with the study—timber-sales procedure and restrictions, for example. Publication on the main aspects of the study is precluded till many years have gone by. Any mistakes made in establishing the study are embalmed in the program and may complicate publication; manuscripts containing either explanations of aberrations or notes of apology find less ready acceptance than manuscripts without them. If a man does not publish regularly, it's hard to promote him. His best chance of publication, and indeed of any research accomplishment while the compartment study is maturing, lies in "side studies" within the framework of the main study or on odd bits of land outside the compartments. Here again, however, he is handicapped, because unless he has more assistants than usually is the case, administering the main study leaves him no time for side studies. The end result is that the Station squanders not only appropriations, but a professional employee.

So it happened in the case of the McNeill Tract. The National Forest Reservation Commission erred in calling the purchase price excessive. The land is of exceptionally high site quality for longleaf pine and was well stocked when we acquired it; by 1962 or 1963, Smith informed me, the current market value of the annual increment exceeded the total purchase price. But the Commission was painfully right about the difficulty and cost of administering a relatively small area so far removed from any other National Forest holding.

The inevitable decision was finally reached in 1963. The Station took down its McNeill Experimental Forest sign and declared the area "surplus," for exchange or other disposition by Region 8. Thanks to site, stocking and Lloyd Smith's skillful silvicultural treatment over many years, the tract is an immensely valuable forest property. The longleaf phenotypes on the area make a geneticist's mouth water at the thought of the genotypes some of them must represent. As a research facility, however, the McNeill Tract has been less an asset than a liability for more than 40 years.

Another second-era change that had far-reaching direct and indirect effects was the transfer of our naval stores research from Starke, Florida, where Len Wyman had started experimental chipping in 1923, to Lake City, Florida, and the present Olustee Experimental Forest.

Starke and Lake City

My picture of this affair is incomplete. I had assisted Wyman at Starke through about a third of the 1925 chipping season and more briefly during 1926, but had had only rather casual contact with him after that. I have not attempted to relate the chronology of the Station's move to Lake City with that of the acquisition of the Osceola National Forest, within which the Olustee Experimental Forest lies, though my recollection is that at least part of the Osceola was purchased before the New Deal. I never saw any of the correspondence relating to the move and never discussed it with either Harper or Wyman, the two men principally affected. In fact, I seem first to have become aware of it on return from annual leave in the summer of 1933, when I heard gossip in the New Orleans Office to the effect that the move was made or to be made and that Wyman, who had joined the Station staff as Associate Silviculturist in 1921, had been demoted to the status of a "hired hand" under Harper, who had joined the staff as Junior Forester 6 years later.

My personal diary for Saturday, September 16, 1933, contains the following entry:

> *Had a talk with Demmie about Len Wyman's predicament Len has failed to carry things through, apparently, and has been deprived of direction and forbidden new projects till he cleans up the Starke work, while Les, who has a flair for administration, develops the Olustee. The action is in effect disciplinary, and intended as such. If Ed² is judging me by Len, as is more than likely he is if only because I've failed to follow through, why, much light is thrown on my own difficulties. Incidentally, Len is very far from being 'merely one of the hired help' to Les, as Station gossip has made him out.*

I thought at the time, and still think, that Len Wyman was treated unjustly in this affair. It is true that he got few of the results of his naval stores research into print. This is not surprising. In those days, one received virtually none of the scheduling, help and guidance characteristic of publishing procedure today. Preparing a manuscript, even if urged by the Director or ordered by Washington, took tremendous individual initiative. Submitting it insured as a rule, criticism, censure and grief; seemingly, none could do anything right.

By failing to publish, Wyman in a sense robbed the Department, the Service, the Station and himself of recognition and credit. Certainly it was argued that he had done so. But, in soundness and utility combined, his research ranked with the growth and yield study that resulted in Miscellaneous Publication 50 and with Lindgren's sapstain control, and outranked most of the early research at the Station, including frankly, my own in artificial regeneration. Furthermore, by direct contact with key men in the naval

---

² Ed Munns, Chief of the Washington Office Division of Silvics. I incurred his displeasure in 1926 or 1927 by citing the Charlie Chaplin alimony in a monthly report to the Branch. He rode me unmercifully through 1936, especially in connection with the U.S. Department Agriculture Tech. Bul. 492, but after a dramatic episode at the 1936 Project Leaders' Conference in Washington, changed front completely.

Len Wyman assigned to the Southern Station in 1921 and was sent to Starke, FL to work on naval stores problems. He was isolated far from most other Station employees, but did some remarkable research.

stores industry, Wyman got his results into practice, and did so I feel sure, more quickly than he could have by whole batteries of publications. In a decade or less, he revolutionized the industry. What he deserved was help with the formal publication phase and credit for accomplishment, not discipline and censure.

As a result, I have no doubt of the discipline that was in fact imposed, Len resigned from the Station in September 1934 and went to teach silviculture at North Carolina State. To this extent, North Carolina State's gain was the Station's loss.

The Starke-Olustee affair; nevertheless, involved large elements of gain for the Station and the Service as a whole. Organizing the Olustee Forest and the new naval stores research at Lake City gave Les Harper scope to prove his ability in research planning, organization and administration and led directly to his Division Chiefship in New Orleans and ultimately to his position as Deputy Chief of the Service.

Improvements in resin production from naval stores trees resulted from advances like reducing the size of the hack and use of chemicals to stimulate gum flow.

Roy Chapman

The appointment of Roy A. Chapman to the permanent staff early in 1929 benefited the Station out of all proportion to all the salary ever paid or credit ever given him.

After his graduation from Minnesota, (in 1927, I think; he had been my Field Assistant at Bogalusa in 1926 before entering his senior year) he had worked on a Forest Service tie sale somewhere in the Rockies. From thence he brought us the story of the colored laborer who had learned to speak Swedish. Most of the laborers on the tie operation were recent immigrants from Sweden who were recruited through a Chicago labor contractor, who had never seen a Negro till they came to this country and who spoke no English. These newcomers the colored linguist would address in tolerably good and quite fluent Svensk. They in turn would hunt up a foreman who spoke their language and ask who the colored man was.

"Oh, he's a Swede."

"*Him* a Swede, with that brown skin and that black wool where he ought to have hair?"

"Oh, yes. It's the climate. You'll look the same way in about 6 months."

It was a rare occasion for which Roy did not have a good story or at least an amusing comment. From the Rocky Mountain tie sale, he went to a cruising job in Minnesota. It was from this job, in what were the depths of winter in the Lake States, that we got him transferred to the Station and it was already spring in New Orleans. When he left the cruising camp in Minnesota, it was 40° below zero. When he arrived in New Orleans less than 3 days later, the temperature was 85°. As Roy put it, he "nearly got up and took off his long woolen underwear right in the dining car."

Roy was one of the most independent, and at the same time, most generously helpful men that ever lived and he was a statistician and an intensely practical one, from skin to marrow. Even during his first 2-1/2 years on the staff, he exerted a strong and stimulating influence in mensurational techniques, experimental design and analytical procedures.

In October 1931, he was detailed to Washington to train under and assist Francis X. Schumacher. The assignment was intended to be of some length but not, I think, as long as it actually lasted, which was a full 3 years. During this period, Roy met and formed a lasting friendship with R.A. (later Sir Ronald) Fisher, whose published works and personal advice did much to shape Roy's own later career.

Roy returned to duty in New Orleans just as the Station got into full swing in new studies and projects arising out of relief financing during the Roosevelt regime. By enthusiasm, know-how and personality, far more than through any formal assignment or authority, he inculcated sound statistical

Roy Chapman coauthored this book on sampling methods with F.X. Schumacher of Duke University. Schumacher was another early leader in the application of statistics to forestry (Schumacher and Chapman 1942).

Wakeley was responsible for establishing the Palustris Experimental Forest for use as an experimental area to evaluate the effectiveness of nursery practices.

procedures in most of the new work started during that lush period. The Southern Station was certainly among the foremost, if not the first, to incorporate such procedures on any such scale; it was generally conceded at the time that it was setting the pace for many of the other Stations. I do not think it is either an exaggeration or an injustice to say that, so far as research proper was concerned, Roy was the real director of the Station's scientific work during this period.

SURFACE PHENOMENA

Better Equipment

Meanwhile, a number of far less important events and innovations caused more stir and brought forth more comments than the really important things like Les Harper's progress and Roy Chapman's return and contributions.

One of these was the transition from Model-T Fords to gear-shift cars. As I recall, this began in 1928 or early 1929 with Siggers' Whippet. And I seem to remember that the Model-T Ford I drove on my nursery survey in December 1929 and which we turned in early in 1930, was our last Model-T. At that, the change to gearshift cars, which coincided with Governor Huey Long's expanding network of paved roads, was by no means unimportant. It brought our centers of

field work nearer. Originally, it had taken 2 days to go from New Orleans to Alexandria and a long 2 days from New Orleans to Urania. By the end of the Second Era, the time was approaching when I could sleep in New Orleans, and by rising early, still keep an 8:00 a.m. appointment with the Supervisor of the Kisatchie National Forest.

Another change was in cameras. The "post-card autographic" Kodaks and the one monstrosity of a long-bellows "view camera" with which we had taken our earliest pictures were at first shoved into the background by, and then altogether abandoned in favor of, two and later three or more Zeiss-Oryx 4- by 6-inch cameras, utilizing pack film.[3] Jimmy Averell, who knew something of cameras, selected the Zeiss-Oryx model and taught a number of us something (though not enough) about using it. They in turn ultimately went by the board. For one thing, they were offsize; film for them became hard to get and finally could be obtained only on special order. We lacked exposure meters too; we used the primitive Harvey meter with windows of varying translucence to indicate the degree of general illumination. Al Bickford under-exposed his pictures badly when using this meter because his pupillary opening was abnormally large and he could read a number or two higher on the meter than anyone else. But the Zeiss cameras were superb instruments and an occasional expert photographer like Tommy Kohara got pictures with them that have been published over and over again. Figure 14B of U.S. Dept. Agr. Agriculture Monograph 18, for example, is a Kohara photo, taken with the Zeiss, that has been used repeatedly in other publications.

---

[3] Compare figures 10 and 11 (Kodak) and figure 18 (Zeiss), and compare figure 57 (Kodak) with figure 59 (Zeiss).

We acquired other useful equipment at intervals during the Second-Era, items that actually cost absurdly little in view of our ambitious undertakings and that seem trivial in this day of photospectrometers and high-speed centrifuges but that carried us many steps forward in several lines of research. One that vastly improved the precision of my own seed studies was our first laboratory Clipper Mill by A.T. Ferrell and Company of Saginaw, Michigan. (It arrived September 24, 1930 and thanks to repeated careful repairs by Norm Scarbrough, it is still in use at the Institute.) As I remember, it cost $32, a price that caused some lifting of eyebrows. Early in my use of it, I discovered that Georgia and South Carolina loblolly seeds seemed to have thicker coats than those from Arkansas and Texas, as evidenced by the greater difficulty of separating full from empty seeds. (This impression of thicker coats was reinforced by Polly Nelson's cutting tests during 1936-1940 and confirmed by micrometer measurements reported in Eyvind Thorbjornsen's doctoral dissertation in 1961. It is a matter of practical importance in specifying seed-cleaning equipment for use in the forest-seed trade.) Carl Hartley got us our first electric refrigerator about late in 1930 or very early in 1931 as a good-will offering in return for our giving Lindgren and Siggers office and laboratory space (which we were under formal agreement to give them anyway). With this one refrigerator, I clinched the effectiveness of cold storage of Southern pine seed, a point hotly debated theretofore by the Washington Office and Polly Nelson later made some studies that revolutionized the whole forest tree seed business and had repercussions throughout the seed trade in general.

Tommy Kohara, a LSU forestry graduate, became a professional photographer.

One lesser item was an express scale for weighing cones, moistening sand to exact specifications, and the like. For slight extra cost, we got scales with a combined English and metric beam and with metric as well as English weights. All the girls who were in the office the day it arrived trooped up to the filthy attic of the Stern Building to weigh themselves. It happened that Patty Bergland was on sick leave that day. When she returned to duty and heard about the scales, she wanted to weigh herself too. Ralph Lindgren, Roy Chapman and I formed a guard of honor to escort her and handed her politely onto the platform without telling her that the units were on the side of the beam away from her and hooked up the appropriate metric weight. She couldn't believe it when the unit she could see indicated that she weighed "51" and was not mollified when we explained that she weighed 51 kilograms. I hope that if Mrs. Lloyd Smith reads this, she won't mind my saying that her then weight of 112.4 pounds was very becoming to her.

Visitors and Local Characters

Wider recognition of our work brought increasing numbers of interesting visitors to the Station, and our expanding program brought contacts with some interesting people in the field.

Alan R. Trist, then a graduate student at Yale, visited the Station during September and October 1928—he nearly knocked me out during a cone-collecting trip west of Slidell by dropping a big slash pine cone on my head—and returned for a briefer stay the following spring with a fellow-Queenslander, a wood technologist named Cecil Ellis. Trist was a brilliant fellow, of half-English, half-Irish descent, who said that the stolid English in him made him walk under ladders just to feel his superstitious Irish hackles rise. Like Australians in general, he was a strong trade unionist. There was a streetcar strike in New Orleans while he was here (never settled, so far as I ever learned; the strikers were simply replaced) and the strikers burned one streetcar up, in front of the Custom House where our office still was at that time. Trist was highly indignant that we didn't all leave our desks and go out and burn up some streetcars also. He had nothing but contempt for the then Prince of Wales, whom he had heard make a good-will speech in Australia and predicted that Edward would "marry a commoner and put himself out of the line of succession." Edward VII did, in fact, marry Mrs. Simpson and abdicate, essentially confirming Trist's shrewd prediction. Trist was, for many years after his visit to us, Secretary of the Queensland Department of Forestry, and in late 1963 or early 1964 became its Conservator General.

Another entertaining Australian visitor, a transplanted Scot named A. Douglas Lindsay, came to us during the Second Era, from the Commonwealth Forestry Bureau at Canberra. At the time, we were in the Stern Building, at the corner of Baronne and Perdido. Doug arrived at night, found the hotel at which a reservation had been made for him (by whom I

The party that met Tor Jonson at Bogalusa on September 18, 1925. From left to right, kneeling: R.D. Forbes, Director of the Southern Station; Roy Hogue, newly appointed State Forester of Mississippi; and W.R. "Billy" Hine, formerly of the Southern Station and here State Forester of Louisiana. Standing: J.K. Johnson of the Great Southern Lumber Company; Louisiana State Ranger Norman Core; Dr. Tor Jonson, then the leading professional forester in Sweden; Harry Lee Baker of the Washington Offices (who became the first State Forester of Florida in 1928); Mr. Johansson (Dr. Jonson's interpreter); Head Ranger F.O. "Red" Bateman of the Great Southern Lumber Co.; and E.L. Demmon, who succeeded Forbes as Director of the Southern Station.

don't know), and retired in too great weariness to assimilate his surroundings. "Imagine my horror," he told us later, "at awaking to find myself in a tin bed!"

His discovery of our office building was amusing, too. He located us approximately by street number, and fetched up directly across Baronne from the building, but at that distance failed to see the rather obscurely lettered name over the door. "Where," he asked a passing New Orleanian, "is the Ster-r-r-n Building?"

"Huh?"

"The Ster-r-r-r-rn Building," repeated Doug, burring his Scott *R* more than ever.

"I don't get you. Could you spell it, Mister?"

"S T E R-R-R-R – N."

"Oh! You mean the Stoin Building!" (Pointing) "It's right over there."

So Doug came in, exasperated Gene Gemmer and me somewhat on a field trip or two (he was an opinionated individual), went on around the United States, returned to Canberra, and produced a flood of little leaflets on American timber species. Though he was amusing, he was not of the same caliber as Alan Trist. Except for his leaflets, I never heard of him again.

Mr. C.H. ("Old Man") Thompson lived alone near Bayou Lacoiana on the south side of the Slidell-Mandeville highway in a little cottage he'd built himself and fitted out with many ingenious and useful gadgets. (Among others, he had a rocking chair that actuated a large and very effective "punkah-type" fan.) I met him first in 1932 through Paul Siggers, who had sprayed a 1-acre longleaf plantation for him to control brown spot. Old Man Thompson was more than 60 then.

He had nearly died of tuberculosis before he was twenty but had recovered during a year or so in Charity Hospital in New Orleans. Discharged with just enough money to buy three muskrat traps, he had lived through the following winter in a hollow sycamore tree and trapped muskrats. His formal education had stopped with the second grade, but he had become educated for practical daily purposes and indeed well read, through his own efforts.

When I first met him, he had acquired perhaps five thousand acres of highly productive second-growth forest land near Bayou Lacombe and was managing it intensively and with a high degree of skill. (He later deeded a square mile of this land to the local 4-H Club.) He had a big magnolia tree, which shed abundant seed and started many seedlings in his strawberry bed; these seedlings he transplanted, grew to suitable sizes and sold to landscapers. One day when I was photographing his longleaf pine plantation, a landscape architect drove up with a special lift truck, said, "Got a 20-foot magnolia, wide-crowned?" and paid the old gentleman $250 cash for the one tree.

Thompson's longleaf pine plantation at age 5 years. He removed all the lateral buds to obtain stem growth without limbs and knots in the wood.

Thompson's longleaf pine plantation at age 18. At age 20, he thinned half for construction of a log home.

Old Man Thompson's original longleaf plantation[*] marked him as the best longleaf planter of us all. The trees averaged 7 feet high at 5 years. He picked off all the lateral buds as high as he could reach and later tweaked off laterals with a screw hook on the end of a long pole. Only one tree in the acre had any branches—or any knots—within 21 feet of the ground. In 1947, when the trees were 20 years old in plantation, he removed half of them in a thinning and sold them to his neighbor, who built a beautiful 5-room log cabin with them.

On October 15, 1930, Mississippi State District Forester N.H. Kimball, took Bob Winters and me to see an amazing forestry operation by W.W. Kurtz near State Line, Mississippi. Kimball himself was a interesting character. His running gun-fight with two men he had previously arrested for incendiarism; his driving out of pistol range and then stopping and wounding one of them with a rifle shot; his reporting the fight to the wrong sheriff through failure to notice he'd crossed a county line; his near conviction March 1, 1930, through perjured testimony, on an attempted murder charge; and his dramatic acquittal when a cousin of the wounded man swore the incendiaries had been chasing Kimball down the road, one man shooting while the other drove, was an epic of the early days of forest-fire control in the Lower South. But, let's get back to Mr. Kurtz.

---

[*] I got good photographs of this plantation, from the same camera point, at ages 5 and 18, but have been unable to obtain prints from Washington. See figure 3 of U.S. Department Agriculture Agriculture Monograph 18, 1954.

W.W. Kurtz grew up on a Central States farm—in Indiana, as I recall, and then for many years ran a successful salmon cannery on the West Coast. Just before World War I, he bought about 2,000 acres, mostly cutover pine land just west of the Mississippi-Alabama line, on which to retire, raise Llewellan setters, hunt quail, and especially train the setters for field trials.

In some way, the details of which I did not inquire, his investments went bad almost immediately and he was left with nothing but an old house, the 2,000 acres of poor land, a small home-canning plant and a Cadillac. He was still making annual trips to the West Coast in the same Cadillac when I met him 17 years later.

With his Indiana or equivalent farm background and his canning plant, Mr. Kurtz made his relatively sterile acres support him and half a dozen tenant families in luxury. Kimball, Winters, and I drove in unannounced. Within 15 minutes, Mrs. Kurtz had hot pot roast (canned) and five or six vegetables on the table. Everything we ate except bread, coffee, sugar, salt and pepper was home-grown. Later, we counted 42 food crops on the place, including a special Irish breed of bacon pigs and an orchard of weird but delicious seedling peaches selected to supply fruit from the very beginning to the very end of the Mississippi peach season. He even had some apples, a fruit not ordinarily grown that close to the Gulf Coast.

I particularly noticed Mr. Kurtz' shotguns. He had two 20-gauge Ithaca doubles, for quail of course. Because his fingers were very thick, he had had these guns made to order, with the left barrel of each semi-choke and the right full choke, the reverse of the usual arrangement. He fired the left barrel first with the rear trigger and had extra space between the front trigger and the front of the trigger guard, to let him get his thick finger it in a hurry. These guns interested me not only intrinsically but because my father-in-law was an inspector in the Ithaca Gun Company. I took down the serial numbers of both guns and got Father Carlson to check them in the records. Sure enough, he had put both of them through the shop and had test-fired them.

How did the impoverished Mr. Kurtz make the money for his annual western trips and his custom-made guns? By intensive management—years of it before he ever knew a profession of forestry existed. (Apparently, he never read anything but gun catalogues and setter stud books and till the day of our visit, he had not known that the United States had a Forest Service.) Yet, by close observation and good common sense, he had transformed 80 acres of merchantable timber and a thousand or so acres of scattered seed trees and worthless oak brush into a lucrative forest property.

He burned the scrub oak for fuel, and reproduced slash and loblolly and even a little longleaf pine all over the area almost at will. He and his tenants kept fire out by connecting the cultivated fields with broad fire-breaks and by pouncing on any accidental or set fire while it was small. He kept the fire-breaks clean by over-grazing them with scrub cattle, confined between temporary fences, and he wore down the rough in the same way to prepare the ground for natural reproduction. He did not sell beef, but if a steer did manage to get fat, he slaughtered and canned it; the pot roast we had enjoyed so much for lunch was just a by-product of his fire-breaks. He made his money selling logs, pulpwood and gum.

When Mr. Kurtz died, he bequeathed his place to the State of Mississippi to form the State Forest which bears his name.

I met Mr. Kurtz only that one time but in my memory, he ranks with Red Bateman of the Great Southern Lumber Company, Professor L.M. Ware of Auburn University, and Old Man Thompson of Bayou Lacombe as among the ablest

silviculturists the South has known. It is an interesting commentary that W.W. Kurtz, a retired salmon canner and Old Man Thompson, a muskrat trapper with only 2 years of formal schooling, should have year after year, scored consistent success at absurdly low cost, in silvicultural operations that still baffle many professionally trained men.

DEFLECTIONS

The Copeland Report

During the Era of Expansion and Recognition, we had our second clearly recognized encounter with a command-performance publication. (In reality, it was the third, as Forbes' "Timber growing and logging and turpentining practices in the Southern Pine Region" was one of a command-performance bulletin series, but as that bulletin was a separate entity, it did not create the emotional pressure of a nationwide publication to which each Station contributed a part.) The first clearly recognized encounter had been with the "Flood Study," which I have already described. This second one was with the so-called Copeland Report and the following excerpts from my personal diary give the flavor of it, I think, better than any more detailed documentation I could dig out of official files.

Monday, February 16, 1931. Staff meeting; the Capper report must be rehashed by May 1.

Friday, July 15, 1932 ... Work on the Copeland resolution threatening to assume the proportions of another flood study; ...

Saturday, July 16, 1932. Received my assignment on the Copeland Resolution report, which will probably take most of my official time till September. The resolution requests that the Secretary of Agriculture inform the Senate whether the Government should undertake to ask the States, in utilizing for forestation, those areas un- suitable for anything else and that he state his reasons and the basis therefore.

Thursday, July 28, 1932. Almost no Copeland conferences.

Friday, August 12, 1932. Mac (H.G. Meginnis) in from Holly Springs, his hands trembling with emotion induced by Ed Munns' outline for the Copeland report.

Tuesday, September 27, 1932 .... got ("my contribution to"— understood) Copeland report stapled and in Bond's hands.

Monday, October 3, 1932. An all-morning session with Demmie (Director Demmon), Walt (Bond) and Cap (Eldredge) with Gene (Gemmer) and Mac (Meginnis) joining in soon after we began, to discuss my section of the Copeland report. Demmie, Walt and Cap called me in primarily to get me to reduce the estimated area needing planting in the shortleaf-loblolly-hardwood type in Georgia, but Mac steadfastly refused to make unwarranted commitments concerning planting needed on drainages he knew nothing about and he and Gene and I

Fire breaks were one of the main management options to protect plantations. Like Kutz, others evaluated using the breaks by disking, fertilizing, and grazing cattle in the areas to reduce hazard development.

hung together on the rest of our figures. One area Cap wanted to reduce on the basis of his ocular impression during a recent trip, Gene increased on the basis of Cap's own crop-meter figures of that same trip. By noon Demmie and Co. were begging me to about double the area they'd previously asked me to cut down. I'm leaving it as it was.[5]

Wednesday, February 1, 1933. All of us in the office went to lunch at the Montelone with Kircher[6], who came down to read a paper of Major Stuart's at the meeting of the Association of Southern Agricultural Workers. After lunch, Kircher told us about the Copeland report...

Monday, February 27, 1933. Demmie back with most encouraging reports about the Copeland work.

The Copeland Report, "A national plan for American forestry", finally came from the Government Printing Office as 73rd Cong. 1st Sess. Senate Doc. 12, in two volumes totaling 1,677 pages. I have little doubt that it bolstered up later constructive legislation—it may even have been instrumental in rescuing our research program from "Depression economy"—but those of us who helped concoct it regarded it less with awe than with ennui. In fact, we were so sick and tired of it that most of us never looked at it. The time devoted to preparing our part of it had made fearful holes in the Southern Station's program for nearly 2 years and the same must have been true of some or all of the other Stations.

Nineteen-thirty saw the publication of Forbes' long overdue, 115-page U.S. Department Agriculture Tech. Bul. 204, "Timber growing and logging and turpentining practices in the Southern Pine Region", with its heavy stress on the evils of fire in any form or for any purpose.

In addition to the reference to the projected forest survey that I have already cited, my personal diary for Monday, April 21, 1930, specifically records a "long staff meeting on fire research."

Nominally, at least, fire research had had top priority in the Station's program ever since the completion of the volume, growth and yield study reported in Miscellaneous Publication 50. The two remaining 1/4-acre Roberts Fire Plots under our charge at Urania, Louisiana, were among the oldest permanent sample plots in the Southern Pine Region, with detailed records going back 16 or 18 years. The 320-acre

Phil Wakeley meeting with Felix Czabator and Phil Briegleb, Director of the Station at the time, in the Director's office. This photo is taken at a time later than the 1932 Copeland report, but illustrates the cooperative nature of the scientific staff.

fire, grazing and natural reproduction study at McNeill, now in its seventh year, was one of our major enterprises and we were becoming concerned about its cost, perhaps by this time, also about continuity of our lease on the study area, and a few of us if the truth be told, about what the data might show. Demmon and Hadley had written a rather caustic review (Jour Forestry 24: 811, 1926) of H.H. Chapman's Yale Forest School Bulletin 16, which had appeared earlier in 1926 and we were in controversy with Chapman on the whole subject of fire and particularly, as I recall, on the interpretation of the data from the Roberts Plots. Demmon was working on the manuscript of what was intended to be a definitive technical bulletin on fire in the southern pine types. All in all, there was plenty of material for a long staff meeting on our fire research.

The South Pasture Report

My personal diary for Wednesday, July 8, 1931, includes the entry: "H.H. Chapman has called the Service's hand on longleaf burning and now we are to be in a turmoil on the fire bulletin."

The "call" almost surely was the statement that Ashley Schiff, in "Fire and water" (Harvard Press, 1962), records as having been "circulated" by Chapman" for professional enlightenment" and to which Robie M. Evans, of Region 7, replied as also recorded by Schiff, on June 20, 1931. Whatever the identity, the routing of Chapman's statement to the Station had the immediate effect of diverting my personal effort from regeneration research to fire studies for the greater part of the next 12 months.

---

[5] For another 13 to 15 years my 1932 estimate remained relatively valid. Then the expansion and intensification of pulp and paper industry operations, together with the post World War II Soil Bank, changed the picture. I suspect that a detailed analysis would show more acres now actually planted than I estimated as in need of planting in 1932, with very large acreages obviously yet to go. And now, with the progress in southern forest tree improvement since 1951, and the large-scale seed orchards, there is talk of clear-cutting stands of good southern pine and replanting the cutover areas with still better man-bred trees.

[6] Joe Kircher became Regional Forester of the Southern Region (Region 8) when it was set up, with headquarters at Atlanta, January 1, 1934. Major Stuart was Chief Forester.

My first reaction to the situation arising from Chapman's challenge was to point out the benefits to be gained by adding to our McNeill and Roberts Plots results the data obtainable from the Great Southern Lumber Company's Longleaf Pine Tract in the South Pasture at Bogalusa.

The plots I had staked out there in the fresh ashes of the 1928 fire had shown within a few months that even a one-square-mile burn did not eliminate brown spot. In the meantime, my original brown-spot spray plots, installed at Carl Hartley's suggestion together with many hundreds of plots laid out later by Siggers, were beginning to show that the effects of the disease on the survival and growth of small longleaf were more serious than we had realized. Lastly, thanks to the Washington Parish Soil Survey and to the Great Southern's maps and other records and to a lesser extent to our own 1925 "Extensive Survey", the logging-, fire- and reproduction-history of the area had been preserved in detail unequalled on any other tract in the South. What I suggested, and what we in fact did, was to compile the available information on the tract and then add to it by counting and measuring seedlings on plots representing all possible combinations of single and multiple burns following seedling establishment and on check plots burned a year and others burned a month before seedfall but not afterwards.

On July 14, 1931, I "completed comments on H.H. Chapman's statement!" On July 15, I "plotted Great Southern's date-of-logging data for the natural reproduction area in the South Pasture at Bogalusa and put some of Hadley's fire data on the same area into usable shape." A note on Sunday, September 13, 1931, reads "revised South Pasture report." Monday, September 14— "To Bogalusa with "Wally" (Wahlenberg), "Frank" Bennett and "(Joe)" Riebold... Talked over details of the South Pasture report with "(Paul)" Garrison and "Red" Bateman, (who knew the area intimately and whose action in getting it fenced in 1921 had saved the longleaf seedlings from hogs) "and then thought out and located, tentatively, 11 of the 18 plots or strips I had suggested in the report."

I spent the greater part of the next 8 or 9 months completing a detailed description and history of the area, including relocation of any unmarked stations from which the Company had taken photographs in 1920. (Relocation involved trampling over the entire ten thousand acres till I recognized old snags, scattered seed trees or odd clumps of brush shown in the original photos. I identified one by a saw-cut partway through an old felled tree top in the immediate foreground. During the winter of 1931-32, several of us including Morrie Huberman (then a Temporary Field Assistant) and myself laid out, ran, staked permanently, tied into section corners and photographed from both ends 18 sample strips, each as a rule, 660 feet long by 6.6 feet wide.

Almost without exception, the longleaf seedlings on these strips were from the bumper 1920 seed crop. Hogs ranging the area prior to fencing in 1921 had cleaned out the seedlings from the big 1913 seed crop. Those from the good 1918 and any from the scant 1919 crop had been killed in the cotyledon

In the early days of southern forest management, prescribed fire was a controversial practice. H.H. Chapman was an early advocate for prescribed fire in southern pine forests, especially for longleaf pine management. But it was a many years before Forest Service scientists agreed that fire could be a beneficial component of forest management.

stage by the early spring burns made to protect turpentine faces and cups. (The Company at that time chipped all old-growth longleaf pine for 2 years before logging.) At the time of the 1920 seedfall, the whole 10,000 acres had supported, at oldest, a 1-year rough developed after the spring of 1920 turpentine burn; 1,500 acres burned over in September 1920 at Austin Cary's suggestion had had a still lighter rough.

The 18 strips represented both conditions of rough at time of seedfall, together with seeding from the side, seeding from overhead in advance of logging, seedfall during logging and skidding and release by logging up to a year after seedfall. Combined with these—through utilization of abandoned and still maintained fire breaks and of accidental single and double burns, were several different histories of exposure of established seedlings to fire; no exposure; a single burn at one or another age; two different combinations of burns at two different ages; annual burns the first 5 years after establishment; and annual burns the first 9 years after establishment.

Hog damage was a major limitation in regeneration of longleaf pine. Seedling roots were a choice food of free ranging hogs, supposedly because of the high nutrient reserves in the large tap roots of this species.

My personal diary for Saturday, April 9, 1932, records that I "Read over the South Pasture report for additions and corrections." On Tuesday, May 24, 1932: "Turned over the text proper of the South Pasture report for preliminary typing." For Thursday, June 23, 1932: "Rewrote my preliminary summary of the South Pasture report for use in Demmie's fire bulletin."

As I recall, this summary for Demmon was really an abstract of the whole report, including the history of the tract and the methods of study. I have no copy of it. The summary and conclusions on pages 56-60 of the "preliminarily typed" text proper read:

Summary and Conclusions

The data contained in this report and in the reports by P.V. Siggers, cited in the appendix, lead to the following conclusions:

1. The outstanding factor responsible for the successful regeneration of longleaf pine over practically the whole 9,485 acres covered in this report was the abundant supply of seed from heavy virgin stands. All other factors play a minor part unless seed supply is taken care of; the best of protection will not insure regeneration on areas where the seed supply is inadequate, as witness thousands of acres of non-restocking protected land bearing scattered seed trees of longleaf pine.

2. Next, after an adequate supply of longleaf pine seed, the most important factor favoring complete regeneration of longleaf pine on the whole tract was the general absence of fire while the seedlings were in the cotyledon stage. There is no authentic record of a burn on any part of the area while the seedlings from the 1920 seed crop were at this fire-sensitive stage of their development.

3. The repeated burning, annual or nearly annual, for many years prior to the seed fall of 1920, must have aided materially in maintaining seed-bed conditions suitable for longleaf pine. It is not impossible to conceive that complete protection for a long period of years before seed fall might have interfered seriously with natural regeneration of longleaf pine.

4. Single fires, fairly light and occurring during the winter months or repeated winter fires or even severe fires occurring as late in the growing season as the third week in March, failed to destroy stands of longleaf pine seedlings 2 years old or older, or to reduce their density below that constituting desirable stocking. (Nine successive fires on the same area did, however, destroy trees to an extent estimated at 65-75 percent, which would have been serious had not the stand originally been overstocked.)

5. Fires after the longleaf pine seedlings became well established (1 to 2 years old, or older) appeared to be intrinsically harmful, in that they increased the mortality, and also delayed height growth except in stands so dense that the increase in mortality resulted in a much needed thinning. Except for this thinning of extremely dense stands, such as occur relatively seldom in the longleaf region as a whole, there is no clear-cut evidence, direct or indirect, that fire has been beneficial to longleaf pine seedlings already established.

6. Fire will not eliminate brown spot or reduce it materially for more than one season under the extreme conditions occurring in T 2 S of the South Pasture Tract, even when the area burned exceeds one square mile in a solid block. (At the time of the observations, there were several thousand contiguous acres densely stocked with even-aged longleaf pine seedlings less than 18 inches high, among which were scattered seedlings up to 10 feet high and capable of retaining some green foliage even in the hottest fire.) An accurate picture of the brown spot situation and its control cannot be obtained by combining infection and injury data from the South Pasture Tract with results obtained by burning portions of smaller areas, less uniformly and densely stocked with trees at the stage most susceptible to brown spot.

7. Brown spot does, under extreme conditions such as occur over large parts of the South Pasture Tract, affect adversely both survival and height growth of longleaf pine seedlings.

8. Even heavy brown spot infection is by no means fatal or even very harmful to young stands of longleaf pine; the best demonstration of this is the 1,200 acres between Knight's Branch and the South Pasture Loop, unburned since establishment, and exhibiting growth of longleaf pine not only excelling that on any other portion of the South Pasture Tract, but equaling any for which records are available.

9. Excessive density of the seedling stand is a limiting factor in height growth, in many instances more important than fire; it is possible that density acts principally through increased brown spot infection. In the South Pasture Tract during the first 11 years of the existence of the young stands, the density at which overstocking begins to exert an adverse influence is approximately 10,000 seedlings per acre.

To summarize even more briefly, brown spot needle blight, if the infected seedlings occur on soil well adapted to longleaf pine, is not the serious inhibiting factor it is sometimes represented to be. The history of the South Pasture Tract does not justify using the presence of brown-spot infection as an excuse for burning.

Further, the South Pasture Tract supports neither the contention that fire is extremely harmful to longleaf pine (except during the cotyledon stage), nor the contention that it is very beneficial to the species or essential to its maintenance on the site. The most appropriate place for fire in the silviculture of longleaf pine would seem to be before logging and seed fall.

If it be argued, in answer to the paragraph above, that the wide separation of the South Pasture plots, the lack of periodic remeasurements of the same plots, together with variations of soil, logging history and so on, obscure the effects of fire (either good or bad), then at least the reply must be admitted that the effects of fire are neither very striking nor very generally obtained.

Demmon accepted my June 23 summary or abstract for incorporation in his fire bulletin manuscript, and for all I know to the contrary, incorporated it. His bulletin died aborning, however; knowledge concerning fire, especially in the longleaf type and policies regarding use of fire and dissemination of information about fire changed so rapidly from 1934 on that the data in the manuscript were hopelessly outmoded and no longer worth printing. My South Pasture report remains in rough draft, on yellow paper. Although re-examination would have yielded a wealth of useful data on both stand structure and brown spot, the 10-chain transects we had examined, monumented and photographed with such care were never re-examined.

The one useful thing that has come out of all my work and that of others on this study has been in the realm of tree improvement. In 1961, Bayne Snyder and Harold Derr used the fire-and-logging maps from my rough-draft report of 1932 to guide them in the selection of putative brown-spot

Harold Derr, silviculturist, did much of the early research in developing brown-spot resistant strains of longleaf pine.

resistant longleaf pines in their half-sib selection study on this subject. They collected cones from the tallest trees they could find, especially in portions of the tract unburned since seedling establishment and with records of 50,000 to 400,000 seedlings per acre 11 years after seed fall. It indeed seems likely that the tallest trees in such areas must include many with exceptional genetic resistance to the disease. Without it, they could hardly have survived, much less made early height growth and become dominant, in the midst of 10,000 acres of dense seedling stands subject to extreme epidemic brown spot for 10 to 20 years.

Two subsequent developments deserve mention in connection with the South Pasture report.

Statements 5 and 6 in the summary of the report proved to be at least partly incorrect. Throughout the 800 acres burned over in the incendiary fire of March 21, 1928, when the seedlings were 7 years old, height growth started a good 3 years earlier than in the adjacent unburned seedling stand. This was clearly the result of decreased brown-spot infection during 1928 and perhaps to a lesser extent during 1929 and thoroughly substantiated Chapman's claim as to the potential value of fire in controlling the disease.

The 100-foot-wide firebreak south of the 1928 burn, at which that fire was stopped, had been burned annually from 1921-22 through 1929-30. Burning was omitted in 1930-31 but with one or possibly two exceptions, the break has been burned every year since. Dr. Risto Sarvas, during his visit to the Station in 1950, was edified at the opportunity of watching the annual burn that winter. As our South Pasture transect work in 1931 showed, the fires had reduced the seedling stand greatly below the 50,000 per acre on the adjacent unburned strip but there were still several thousand per acre. The Company subsequently made several pulpwood thinnings on the annually burned break and in 1964 reaped a handsome profit by thinning the burned stand for poles. After more than 40 burns, beginning when the seedlings were 1 year old, the burned break supports a nearly ideal stand of longleaf pine.

I had planned to detail here the preparation, evidently vigorously under way in 1933, of Wahlenberg, Greene and Reed's bulletin manuscript on the McNeill study. This finally appeared in June 1939 as U. S. Department Agriculture Tech. Bul. 683, "Effects of fire and cattle gazing on longleaf pine lands, as studied at McNeill, Mississippi." I have already noted its background, however, in connection both with the establishment of the study and with the purchase of the McNeill Tract and I find that on pages 79-81 and elsewhere in his "Fire and water" (Harvard University Press, 1962), Schiff has given an excellent account of this bulletin's checkered career. Schiff was able to draw on historical sources to which I have never had access, and is I think, scrupulously fair with regard to this publication. He states: "That the bulletin ever appeared can be largely attributed to Wahlenberg's perseverance," and this I can confirm from close personal contact with Wahlenberg during the period concerned.

PERSONAL PREOCCUPATIONS

Flops and Failures

Confessedly, my personal outlook and experience, bias this history. And for that reason, I make no bones about recreating the "feel" of the Second Era in terms of my own failures and successes.

In connection with Pessin's very popular Occasional Paper on sodium-arsenate killing of unwanted hardwoods, I have mentioned my own 1929 attempt to poison scrub oaks at Upper Coburn's Creek by inserting toxic solutions in auger holes in the bases of each of five oaks. One solution gave a partial kill, the other four chemicals were ineffective, I had other things to do and I abandoned this impromptu and informal study. Had I made a real literature search, drawn up a "problem analysis" (for which I had ample perspective from observation of brushy planting sites), got Station support and persisted, I might have anticipated Pessin's success—perhaps, later repeated the study with post-World-War-II chemicals and anticipated Peevy's success with Ammate. Had I done so, I would have had a real "breakthrough" and a substantial accomplishment to my credit. I have come to realize though, that any reasonably busy man's career is studded with such lost opportunities. This wasn't my only one.

At the Parsons Nursery Conference in West Virginia in August 1931, I met for the second time a Dr. Stewart who, (after as I recall, some successful research on pineapples in Hawaii) had been hired by the Northeastern Station to study the soil properties and other underlying causes of plantation successes and failures in New York and the New England States. After 2 years of work, in which he compiled all available data on approximately a thousand plantations, he found that the records on establishment and later treatment were so meager and incomplete for all but about six, that the study had to be abandoned.

This gave me an idea. By the spring of 1926, the Great Southern Lumber Company had planted 12,700 acres on which I could salvage, or in most instances already had (in connection with the Hayes-Wakeley bulletin of 1929), all pertinent data, including geographic source of seed. Virtually all the other planting in the South had been done since 1926 by four other companies whose records I could get or by farmers whose stock from State nurseries I could trace; in particular, Hux Coulter in Florida, was filling in a form with systematic early re-examinations on every plantation made with State stock. A few older plantations had also been well documented, mostly by W.R. Mattoon. If I took advantage of this timely start, I could compile a set of records that, a pulpwood rotation later, would not have to be discarded as inadequate. The records could easily be extended to include a thousand plantations and some of the individual

Fred Peevy did pioneering research on the use of herbicides to kill undesirable hardwoods on pine sites. The results of his research was applied across the South.

plantations would be square miles in extent. As source arterial for plantation success or failure or growth and yield studies, the records would be without peer. My personal diary for Thursdays July 28, 1932, in addition to the ironic note "Almost no Copeland conferences," includes the entry:

> Got down to work and outlined the working plan for Fp1, Inventory of Federal, State and Private Plantations. Actually, this is the first formal working plan I've ever prepared for the Station—all my work so far has been on projects laid out by other men—and I'm as excited as a girl about to be kissed for the first time.

This plantation inventory—unlike the little brush poisoning study and a number of other informal studies—I managed to have included in the Station's established program. It attracted favorable attention inside and outside the Service. I designed forms for it, (quite good ones, if I do say so myself), set up files for it, compiled all pertinent data available at the Station, abstracted published descriptions of plantations (we had no Xerox then!) and described plantations myself as field trips offered opportunity. I made one special trip to Tallahassee to copy a lot of Coulter's records. In 1937, we used ECW money to hire a chap named Joiner, who traced records of and described in the field, and very competently so, a number of plantations in several States.

In the changeover from functional to territorial research after World War II, however, while I was writing Agriculture Monograph 18, this Plantation Inventory study got lost in the shuffle and died by default. Like so much research in artificial regeneration, it didn't fit into the program of any one

Research Center well enough to attract the Center Program Leader or staff. A few of the records of individual plantations proved useful when need for them came to my attention; if I had a record at all, my files permitted prompt retrieval. Several times, in connection with recent genetics research, I have been able to authenticate geographic sources of seed from the records of this study. In one instance, I was able to supply a copy of an experimental plantation establishment report to a Forestry School that had lost the original. I still think the inventory was soundly conceived, but it's dead. When it comes to a really authoritative study of plantation success and failure or growth and yield, we are in exactly the same unfortunate position today that bedeviled the Northeastern plantation 35 years ago.

In the course of my re-examinations of the plantations at Bogalusa, I had formed the impression that the smaller seedlings of all southern pines started growth earlier in the spring than the larger ones. By late 1929, I had become curious about the relation of this phenomenon to infection of longleaf pine by brown spot. In February 1930, accordingly, I classified the buds of about 200 longleaf seedlings, 4 years in plantation, as "pincushion," "round brown," "round white" and "cylindrical" or "elongated." The smallest seedlings had flat, naked or nearly naked buds in which the exposed tips of the new needles did indeed resemble cushions full of pins. The largest, though still not more than an inch tall, had cylindrical buds up to an inch long, with the heavy white scales characteristic of the buds on seedlings that had already emerged from the "grass stage" and these seedlings appeared ready to start height growth during 1930. At bi-weekly intervals or thereabouts during the spring of 1930, I recorded the average length of the new needles on each of these seedlings and noted any evidence of brown-spot infection.

This was another "informal," exploratory or impromptu study, without a written plan and not recorded in the Station's

Longleaf pine buds in the "elongated" category.

official program, but it was an absorbingly interesting one. My personal diary includes the following notes concerning it:

Thursday, March 13, 1930. Finished second longleaf phenological examination; the seedlings with poor buds are still coming out ahead of the others, such needles as are out have elongated about 1 cm. since Sunday morning and several seem already infected.

Monday, April 14, 1930. Practically completed rough computation of data to date on phenological examination of spring-planted longleaf, 1925-26, at Bogalusa. The most clear cut and satisfactory data I've handled since I've been at the Station. There's no doubt possible about the smaller seedlings coming out first in the spring or about their getting infected first with brown spot.

A later examination showed the brown-spot organism actually existing on 1930 foliage of "pincushion" seedlings before the last of the "cylindrical-bud" seedlings had any 1930 needles out of the buds and exposed to brown-spot infection.

Saturday, April 11, 1931. Made a detailed phenological re-examination of the spring-planted longleaf 25-26 used for the phenological study last year. Incidentally, that study should have been in print by now and it isn't even written up.

It should indeed have been in print. Its implications for nursery and planting practice, for prevention and use of fire in longleaf management and for brown-spot control, were far reaching and important. I like to think that my frequent verbal reports of the findings were some good. By hand-sorting of data from the routine 15-year re-examination made of the plantation in 1941, my stalwart helper, Reva Thielen, was later able to show that all the cylinder-bud seedlings had lived but that more than 20 percent of the pincushion-bud seedlings had died and that cylinder-bud seedlings averaged 18 feet tall as against only 1.5 feet for the surviving pincushion-bud seedlings (U.S. Department Agriculture Agriculture Monograph, 1954, figure 49). Aside from this publication in Agriculture Monograph 18, I never *have* gotten a publication of the study. Oh, well, "Man is not puffick," as the old Negro said when haled before the same judge for the thirty-eighth time for chicken stealing.

Partial Successes

Not all my spontaneous research efforts ended as dismally as the Plantation Inventory and the longleaf bud study.

In the winter of 1930-31, it dawned on me from observation from miscellaneous reading and from discussion with specialists in other fields, that: (1) the chief weakness of our sandflat germination tests was the difficulty of maintaining optimum moisture supply; (2) filter-paper substrates, under covers, kept moisture more nearly at optimum level than did sand but served as hotbeds for molds, which over-ran the seeds also; (3) molds and other fungi, many of which grew best on neutral substrates and some at least of which: decomposed cellulose, were only to be expected on filter paper; and (4) acid, granulated moss peat promised to supply moisture even better than filter paper and its low pH might impede development of fungi. The sequence of events, thereafter as recorded in my personal diary, was sketchily as follows:

Tuesday, January 20, 1931 ....Made acid peat substrate for chamber tests.

Wednesday, January 28, 1931. Fresh longleaf seed on peat moss reached 68% germination on seventh day.

Wednesday, February 3, 1932. Seed equipment all day; built the square peat mats and they promise very well.

Thursday, February 26, 1932 ....Also, worked with Ted Coile on moss pads.

Friday, February 27, 1932. Ted is turning out perfect moss cakes.

Monday, June 13, 1932 ....wrote a note for 'Science' on the use of the peat mat.

Thursday, June 16, 1932. Miss Kerr edited my note for 'Science' on peat mats.

I grant that this was "applied" rather than "basic" research, so I dealt merely with a problem of "facilitating techniques," and the total effort involved was small, but I have known the efforts to drag to a slower end or reach no end at all. From evaluation of the problem to final publication took less than 2 months and publication was in a reputable journal. The "note" of my June 13, 1932, diary appeared in *Science* 76 (1933): 627-628, for June 16, 1932. It was, incidentally, my one and only contribution to that august periodical.

Ed Munns promptly inquired of me, personally, whether I had taken time to get a public patent on the peat mats to prevent their exploitation for private gain and reprimanded me because I had failed to do so. In the light of riper experience, I have come to think that it is the Director's responsibility to foresee any such danger and constitute patent proceedings. I also question whether the mats are patentable. Certainly nobody ever exploited them for private use.

As far as I know, nobody except my various assistants and I ever tested my peat mats. From 1933, however, until World War II terminated the Station's service testing of seed for the Federal and State nurseries in Region 8, the peat mat was the standard substrate for germination tests of southern pine seed. All Polly Nelson's work on seed storage hinged on peat-mat germination. Her classic research on light requirements of southern pine seed, still being cited both in this country and abroad as recently as 1964, not only revealed a previously unsuspected advantage of mats over sandflats in the matter of light supply but owed its very inception to the stacking

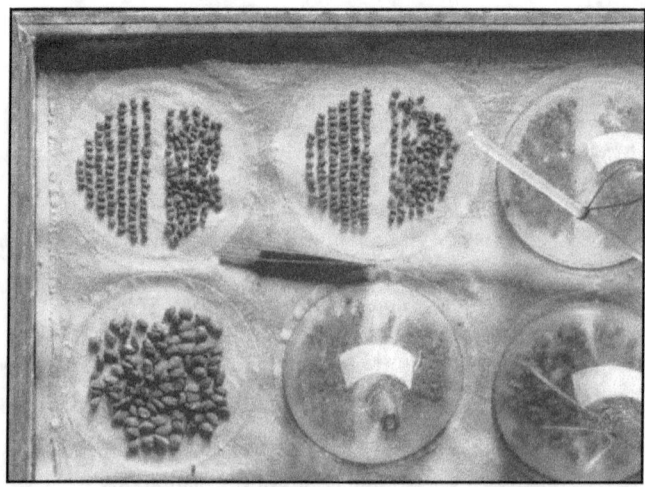

This is the germinator that had mold development on the filter-paper substrate that adversely affected germination.

of some mats to save laboratory space. It was not till after World War II that the mats were superseded by the open-face, covered-dish, sand-vermiculite substrate originated by Maki, further developed by Bob Allen and perfected by and now standard at the Macon and Alexandria seed laboratories.

By the time the 1930 seed crop was out of the cones, several of us, notably Gemmer, Wahlenberg and I, had become exercised over the periodicity of southern pine seed production. As I recall, some trapping of longleaf seed by Wahlenberg in cumbersome 1-square-milacre board and wire frames at McNeill, had given us food for thought. I remember distinctly that we three had begun to question the then generally accepted dogma that longleaf seeded regularly every seventh year. At the same time, I was irked by what I considered the lack of technical professional activity by the rather recently formed Gulf States Section of the Society of American Foresters.

My personal diary for Friday, March 13, 1931, records an afternoon meeting of the Gulf States Section in the Station office and an evening "banquet" and business meeting at the Jung hotel and concludes: "Successfully floated a motion for an intersection committee on cone reporting." As so often happens, the man who moved the appointment of the committee was appointed chairman. My diary entries continue:

Wednesday, May 13, 1931. Sent proposed cone crop reporting forms to chairmen of Ozark, Washington, Appalachian and Southeastern Sections.

Monday, June 29, 1931. Cone crop report forms about ready to send out. Lots of correspondence concerning them and Ed Munns has been appointed by the Washington Section to act on our committee!

The exclamation mark above is a direct quotation from my diary entry. As Ed was in line authority over me and was

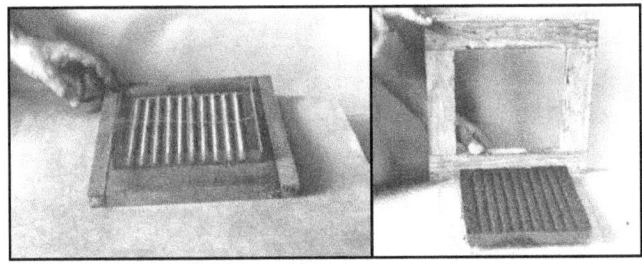

Peat mats were an improved germination medium for pine seeds. On the left is the equipment that Wakeley developed to form peat mats (drill mold, wire border, and moist peat). On the right is a mat being removed from the frame. Seeds would be placed in the drill rows for germination.

systematically and officially "riding" me at the time, it was only human on my part to be tickled at having him assigned under my chairmanship. I was never able to trace any cone crop report to his efforts, however.

Saturday, August 29, 1931. Arrived New Orleans at 9:45...To the office, where there were enough cone crop reports waiting to bring our numbers of reporters to about 45 and our individual species reports to about 110. Straightened out reports and also various notes on trip.

Tuesday, September 1, 1931. Mailed cone crop reports (estimates, rather) to all local reporters and to all members of the Gulf States Section not attached to the Southern Station.

That first mimeographed estimate was 10 single-spaced pages long. It gave, separately by species, the cone production by localities covered by reporters, logging operations expected to be in progress on bearing stands when cones were mature, the names and addresses of local collectors and the locations of stands considered especially desirable as sources of seed. Even then we were feeling our way toward the modern concepts of "plus" stands and of seed production areas.

We made a second estimate in 1932, a poor seed year. It included 88 reports from 42 reporters. In 1932 as in 1931, only Society members were solicited for reports and report forms and the estimates compiled from them were mailed under stamp, with postage paid by the Gulf States Section. Gulf States Section dues in those days were, if I remember correctly, only 25 cents a year and the 1931 and 1932 mailings, plus the paper used, practically exhausted the Section treasury.

Saturday, February 4, 1933. Gulf States Section meeting in the morning. Items:...my getting the cone crop committee continued, but only after some persuasion.

The Civilian Conservation Corps was created the summer after that meeting, and in the South especially, its emphasis was on forest planting in addition to fire fighting and construction work. To help cope with the demand for seed expected in connection with the Corps' program, the Station took over the cone crop estimate—primarily to increase (by

use of the franking privilege) the number of report forms that could be sent out.

I continued to conduct the estimate, at first with clerical help only, but from 1936 through 1939 with technical assistance from Polly Nelson and in 1940 from Earl Stone. We greatly improved the report forms; eventually we got fair estimates of annual cone production, over large portions of the South, in terms of bushels per acre. In 1936, we illustrated the estimates with crude maps; in 1937-1941 with respectably neat ones. In 1940, we rose to the dizzy heights of 882 reports from 230 reporters. The last estimate was made in 1941, during the Defense Period just before Pearl Harbor, and the increasing provision of manpower to defense cut the number of reporters to 143 and of reports to 599.

World War II terminated the cone crop estimates and we were unable to resume them. Post War Station policy could not condone them as research and the report forms, moreover, were "questionnaires" in the eyes of Bureau of Budget personnel, without whose approval we could no longer send them out.

Several interesting and amusing things happened during or grew out of the 11 years' cone-crop estimating.

Much the best and most reliable estimates were made by CCC Camp Project Superintendents. Collecting cones was, in many instances, an important part of their work. Some of them developed an uncanny capacity to tell how many bushels could be collected on an acre. Furthermore, they spent so much time filling out forms of all kinds that they took our cone crop forms in stride. Much the poorest reports were

This S-shaped cone hook made cone collection from standing trees much more efficient.

CCC "boys" unloading sacks of pine cones collected from standing trees and placed in cone drying buildings. These facilities were located at the Stuart Nursery camp near Pollock, LA. The cones were kilned and seeds were dried and stored for use at the nursery.

turned in by my colleagues on the Southern Station staff—if they bothered to report at all. (Knowing me personally, they stood in no awe of me; a prophet is not without honor save in his own country!) Almost to a man the Southern Station reporters altered the crucial headings on the forms, rendering the reports useless for statistical processing.

As the expansion of the CCC program increased the demand for seed, more and more orders were placed with the local collectors we listed in the estimates. Some men who collected and extracted seed with care established good reputations and eventually got orders from unexpected sources. One day a young farmer named Waldo Brown, who lived near Picayune, Mississippi, wandered into the office and asked if the New Zealand Forest Service was "good for its debts." I assured him it ought to be and asked if he'd had any trouble with that organization. He said no, but they'd just cabled him an offer of $5.00 a pound for 200 pounds of slash pine seed and he wanted to check up before he collected that much. He collected and shipped the seed—we learned later from New Zealand that it had arrived in good condition and was of excellent quality— and received prompt payment. With his profits, he paid off the mortgage on his farm and got married!

We included in the annual estimates not only the names of local collectors but also those of established dealers whose catalogues listed southern pine seed. As a matter of courtesy, we sent copies of the estimates to such dealers. One year, I forget just which, we got a violent reaction from Herbst Brothers of New York, which we assume was prompted by the fear that through our listing of local collectors, someone would get to *their* collectors and offer better prices. Herbst Brothers ordered us to abandon the estimates. When we

declined, diplomatically to do so, they threatened to go to their congressman and get the whole Forest Service abolished. The very next year, however, the cone crop failed in the locality from which they had been getting their southern pine seed and they wrote us a humble and apologetic letter asking for a copy of the current estimate.

One established dealer with whom our relations were cordial from the start was Richard V. Bausher of Allentown, Pennsylvania. He always acknowledged the estimates we sent him, with thanks for listing his firm and after the War, he urged us repeatedly to re-establish the cone-crop-reporting service. We explained why we were unable to do so and as late as 1963, received a letter from him, expressing appreciation of our earlier work and wishing we might resume it.

Abandonment of the estimates was an unavoidable wartime economy and it scotched my original dream of building up an accurate picture of zones and periodicity of seed production of southern pines. I still think the project was legitimate and essentially basic research, not "mere service" as the Station officially classified it after the War. We learned much from the 11 estimates we made; crude, sketchy and incomplete though the first two were.

In 1937, for example, northcentral Florida produced 10 times as much longleaf seed per acre and the northeastern Florida flatwoods produced 100 times as much per acre as the deep sands of western Florida. Abundance of longleaf seed that year was strikingly associated with major soil provinces. Whether one is intent on reproducing stands naturally or is minding his *p's* and *q's* with regard to the provenance of seed for artificial regeneration, such information about seed production is an asset. It would be helpful, too, in deciding where to establish seed orchards.

It was clear also from the 11 successive annual estimates that loblolly pine was not the universally frequent and prolific seeder described in the literature. The way the erroneous picture had become embalmed in print is interesting and should be a warning to research organizations. The published observations on loblolly seed production had been made by Cope in Maryland, Ashe in North Carolina (especially eastern North Carolina), Mattoon in eastern South Carolina, and most recently, by myself at Bogalusa, Louisiana. All these areas are coastal or near-coastal, and as the cone-crop estimates showed, loblolly does seed abundantly and often in these places. But throughout the inland, three-quarters of its range, loblolly seeds much less well. During the 11 years the SAF-Station estimates were made, there was not a single good crop of loblolly seed in Texas.

This pattern of loblolly seed production was the one result of the 11 estimates clear and definite enough to justify a technical article and I had such an article in mind when, in 1947, H.H. Chapman wrote to me personally, asking a number of penetrating questions about loblolly seed. I replied with a narrative description; in general terms and including the Cope-Ashe-Mattoon item and the Texas example just mentioned but none of the analytical data I planned to use in the article. Rather, to my consternation, H.H. sent my letter to the *Journal of Forestry*, which published it verbatim over my signature (Vol. 45, pp. 676-677, 1947), as a letter and an article. This put me in the peculiar position of having stolen my own thunder and I never wrote the technical article. Net result, 11 years' sizable effort, unknown to the present generation of the Station staff, with no indexed publication to show for it.

I'm still rather proud of the old cone crop estimates, however. I've had immediate practical results, like helping State Foresters and established seed dealers find seed and getting Waldo Brown married and they improved our overall picture of seed production. With them, moreover, I learned the technique of extending research to the limits of financial allotments and the formal boundaries of the Station territory, by interesting other people in a regional technical problem and enlisting their cooperation to solve it. In 1951, when I had only 6 days' travel expenses and $20 for equipment and supplies for the Station's whole genetics program, I used the same technique to launch the Southwide Pine Seed Source Study, which is now one of the major activities of the Institute of Genetics.

U.S. Department Agriculture Tech. Bul. 492, published in 1936 under a 1935 deadline, contains the cautious statements that: "Cold storage, according to the results of recent tests, keeps all species of southern pine seed in good condition for at least 1 or 2 years" and an unknown factor—such, perhaps as moisture content of the seed if it is placed in storage—has a marked effect on keeping quality." The wording was the Washington Office's conservative toning down of a more forthright recommendation in my original manuscript. Why cold storage seemed such heresy to the Washington Office, I don't know. Later, of course, Lela Barton at Boyce Thompson Institute and Polly Nelson and I at the Station proved to the hilt the efficacy of cold storage combined with low seed moisture content and the stock lot from which a slash pine sample mentioned in the following quotations was drawn, germinated 84 percent after refrigeration for 30 years.

I first placed seed in cold storage in the fall of 1927, after sealing at air temperature, treating seed with formaldehyde before storage and several other treatments wide of the physiological mark had given negative results. The following excerpts from my personal diary chronicle the early successes with the method that the Washington Office questioned in 1934-35.

Loblolly pine pulpwood produced at Bogalusa, LA after planting seed sources from Louisiana, Texas, Georgia and Arkansas in 1925. The yields of pulpwood were 42, 23, 18, and 15 cords per acre for the four sources after 22 years. This study indicated the potential of improving productivity by selecting seeds from particular sources and led to the development of other tree improvement programs.

Friday, January 31, 1930. Fresh longleaf and 2-year- old cold storage longleaf have started on the tenth and ninth day, respectively.

Tuesday, February 4, 1930. Germination counts; fresh longleaf and both cold storage lots of longleaf (1 and 2 yr.) are doing well...

Wednesday, January 28, 1931. Longleaf stored a year at low temperature at the Lake States Station, both in paper and in sealed glass, started to germinate the ninth day in sand.

The reference to storage at the Lake States' Station is revealing. We had no refrigerator of our own, could arrange for none in New Orleans and had to farm out our cold storage tests among more fortunate colleagues. The 2-year-old cold storage longleaf referred to in the January 1930 excerpt above was the second of five refrigerated at Louisiana State University through the courtesy of Gordon Marckworth of the School of Forestry. Unfortunately, his students found that longleaf seeds were as tasty as pinon nuts and ate all the 3-, 4-, and 5-year lots.

Monday, March 21, 1932. Worked on seed samples all day; put 10 years' supply of longleaf, slash, loblolly and shortleaf in cold storage, with checks at room temperature...

These lots were in 1-pint glass Mason jars in the refrigerator obtained for us by Carl Hartley. We used a separate jar for each species for each period of storage because we had begun to suspect that taking a container out of refrigeration and opening it to remove test samples, affected the seed adversely; we later showed this to be true in some cases. Surplus seed of slash pine was stored cold in a separate sealed glass jar. Results with these lots formed the background of Polly Nelson's Occasional Paper 78, "Preliminary investigations on dry, cold storage of southern pine seed and of her Successful cold storage of southern pine seed for seven years" (Journal Forestry 38: 444, 1940). The residue of the slash surplus was still germinating well after 30 years as when first collected.

After World War II, B.F. McLemore initiated a number of studies of southern pine seeds related to storage. This significant seed research program was established at the Alexandria Forestry Center.

Hybridization

As the Primitive Era gave way to the Era of Expansion, I began to play around with controlled crosses of various pine species.

My first attempt was to authenticate the longleaf x loblolly parentage of Sonderegger pine by producing this hybrid artificially. (Not until 1952, however, by Hoy Grigsby in Mississippi, 1953, by Roland Schoenike at Crossett and 1954, by Allen and Scarbrough at the Harrison Experimental Forest and by Tucker Campbell and myself at Many, Louisiana, was Sonderegger pine produced by controlled pollination.) My first official diary entry on the subject reads:

Tuesday, March 20, 1928. Climbed longleaf and loblolly pines near the nursery in the afternoon and sacked pistillate flowers of both species for possible hybridizing tests. Lots of fun.

This was at Bogalusa, the nursery was the Great Southern's and the sacks were kraft paper. When I resumed controlled pollination in earnest in 1954, at Many, Louisiana with Tucker Campbell, artificial hybridization still appealed to me as one of the best of outdoor sports and I fully intend to continue it in New York State after retirement.

I pollinated the bagged flowers on (longleaf) breeding tree No.1 and (loblolly) breeding tree No. 2 on Saturday, March 24, 1928, those on each with pollen from the other tree. The attempt failed. The control-pollinated loblolly strobili aborted

Bagging of longleaf pine flowers in a hybridization study.

early and cone insects got all the control-pollinated cones on the longleaf tree by October 1929, together with all but one wind-pollinated cone on the same tree.

In all, I pollinated in 3 years–1928, 1929 and 1930 on trees 1 and 2 and once in 1931, on a Sonderegger pine discovered by J.K. Johnson in "Automobile Holler" on the highway to Franklinton. Two of the four attempts succeeded. Slash pine pollen collected at Slidell, Louisiana on February 16, 1929, and applied March 13 to flowers bagged on longleaf breeding tree No.1 on February 17, yielded six cones on October 16, 1930. (The seeds from each individual cone were carried in the records under a separate seed lot number.) Controlled pollinations made in March 1931 on the Sonderegger pine in "Automobile Holler" yielded on October 14, 1932, three cones from selfing, two from back-crossing with loblolly pollen and five from back-crossing with longleaf pollen.

Saturday, March 7, 1931. Put in seed in City Parking Commission Nursery, a sticky place if ever there was one.

It was *Parkways* Commission, not "Parking." Borrowed facilities again, as for seed storage! We had no experimental nursery in 1931; the Depression was upon us and reduction of operating funds precluded driving the 80-odd miles to Bogalusa and incurring subsistence while there, to do nursery research. The Washington Office, moreover, had decided that after 2 years of Hadley's "forestation" research and 6 of mine, the Station had learned all there was to know about artificial regeneration of southern pines. But I was bound and determined to progeny-test my control-pollinated seed and took any avenue I could to that end. I arranged for the nursery space through Mr. George Thomas, head of the Parkways Commission, whom I had met through the New Orleans Botanical Society.

Saturday, April 4, 1931....three lots of hybrid seed coming up.

Sunday, April 19, 1931. Some of the slash–longleaf crosses are certainly hybrid in appearance.

They were properly longleaf x slash, of course, but I had not yet talked enough with geneticists to have learned that the female parent is mentioned first. The seedlings were indeed hybrids, the first of any southern pines made under control and according to "Pete" Righter, the third authentic artificial crosses of my pine species. Three survived the glutinous rigors of the City Parkways Commission's nursery and I planted them in the "Arboretum Half-Acre" at Coburn's Creek, Bogalusa. One died the first summer. A second proved excessively susceptible to brown spot and died about 4 years after it was planted. The third, though rust colored about 20 feet above the ground, throve, and developed into a tree of fine form. In fact, the canker was arrested and largely grew over—a longleaf-parent rather than a slash-parent trait. The canker made a weak spot, however, and about 1956 the trunk snapped into at this point in a windstorm and the tree died, less than a week before I drove to Bogalusa to take my first color photograph of it.

So passed our only Southern Station specimens of my first artificial hybrids. Fortunately, we had shared seed, even-Stephen, with Eddy Tree Breeding Station at Placerville, which, as the (Western) Institute of Forest Genetics, still had some 16 specimens of the original longleaf x slash cross in its Eddy Arboretum at the time of my last visit there in 1959.

Note the recurrence of Saturday (afternoon) and Sunday dates in the diary excerpts above. I sowed and examined the hybrids on my own time. I had made the pollinations after office hours, too— that is, after 5 o'clock. This was less because the air was quiet at that hour than because Washington overhead disapproved of what I was doing. I was criticized for "dissipating my efforts" even on my own time. Yet, after the hybrids were published (by Ernst Schreiner, in the 1937 Yearbook of Agriculture), the same man who voiced the criticism wanted to know why the hell I hadn't made more of them!

This longleaf pine had an important role in the longleaf breeding program. Known as "Father Abe", this tree was identified in an abandoned nursery bed as being resistant to brown-spot needle disease. It was planted in the late 1930s on the Palustris Experimental Forest and was hybridized with a number of other pines that had partial resistance to brown-spot disease. The tree was killed by lightning in the early 1980s, but a number of clones exist.

The seed from the 1931 controlled pollinations on the Sonderegger pine in "Automobile Holler" yielded one back-cross to loblolly and one to longleaf pine, which I planted in the Arboretum Half-Acre at Coburn's Creek. The loblolly back-cross eventually died from multiple cankering by fusiform rust. The longleaf back-cross, though suppressed until 1958 by a neighboring Sonderegger pine planted in 1926-27, still survives, the only artificial hybrid in the Station's experimental plantations at Bogalusa.

It was on the strength of these early efforts, plus the acre of loblolly seed-source plantation at Bogalusa, plus an abortive seed-source study undertaken in 1935, that I became the Station's original "expert" or "specialist" in forest genetics and that the Station's genetics program was dumped into my solitary lap in 1950-51.

TECHNICAL BULLETIN 492

During 1929, I forget just when or how, the idea developed that I should write a bulletin on the results of our seed, nursery, and planting research. (I was at the time an Assistant Silviculturist, then equivalent to today's GS-9, at something less than $2,900 a year.) The Station was under pressure to wind up its program in these subjects, on which it was assumed we now had all the answers[7] and made my time available for more useful work.

I had reservations about the completeness of our results, especially in the nursery. My first move, as plans for the bulletin took shape, was a survey of six nurseries—L.S.U. Forest School at Baton Rouge; Division of Forestry at Woodworth, Louisiana; Industrial Lumber Company at Elizabeth, Louisiana; Long Bell Lumber Company at DeRidder, Louisiana (at which I first met A.D. Read); and Texas Forest Service Nurseries at Kirbyville and Conroe.

---

[7] The Station's Ninth Annual Report, for 1929, says: "As already stated, the problem of reforesting the millions of acres of denuded and understocked forest land in the South is considered one of paramount importance to the future well being of the entire region… There are…at least 10 million acres of longleaf pine land where new forest stands can be grown only by artificial measures. An additional area of 20 million acres is producing but a fraction of its possible forest growth, which can be increased substantially only by forest planting. The demand for information on nursery and planting practices becomes more pronounced each year as the acreage planted to forest tree seedlings in the South increases… For instance, no successful method has been found for holding over longleaf seed to be used for planting in the poor seed years which normally follow good seed crops…"

"The Station has had one man spending practically his entire time on forestation projects ever since the Station was established…" (a period of 8-1/2 years, the first 4 years of which yielded 4 acres of spacing plantations established, and no publications whatsoever. P.C.W.)

From these premises, in the non-sequitur of the time, the Ninth Annual Report concludes: "The forestation program of the Southern Station should, therefore, show no expansion. It *may* (underscore mine. P.C.W.) "be advisable to observe currently the main commercial forestation projects throughout the South."

These six, with the Great Southern Lumber Company nursery at Bogalusa, were almost the only nurseries worth mentioning in the South and I had already known the Great Southern's operation intimately for 5 years.

I could write a whole book on that 9-day, 1,200-mile trip. I made it in one of our original 1924 Model-T Fords—the one Lentz and Putnam had used in the Bottomland Hardwood Survey. It had 70,000 miles on its all-too-frequently disconnected speedometer, made 8 miles to the gallon, rarely attained 20 miles an hour and at one point, subjected me to the ignominy of being overtaken on the open road by a horse and buggy. Its curtains were in tatters and during the trip, there was an unprecedented freeze. When I got back from the trip, we turned the car in for $12.50 toward a new car.

My nursery reconnaissance was highly successful despite the hardships imposed by the decrepit car and the hard freeze. From my familiarity with the seed extraction and nursery practices of the Great Southern at Bogalusa, I was able to provide myself in advance with typed outlines of headings covering almost every conceivable phase of equipment and work. Each of the nurseries I visited was in charge of an observant, ingenious, uninhibited man or men—Marckworth, the Delaney Brothers, Earl King, Read, Bean, Budde. Environment and facilities differed greatly from nursery to nursery; problems and ways of solving them differed even more. From that one trip, rather than from our inept and trifling nursery studies at Bogalusa, I learned enough to write a passable treatise on nursery practice. I have kept to this day the reports I filled out at the various stops; they have been useful as recently as 1964 in authenticating the geographic source of seed in several important plantations.

I never dreamed, when I started it, how much difficulty, frustration and heartache writing that bulletin would involve. My first personal diary entry regarding it (though it records yet another instance of work on my own time) was certainly jaunty and cheerful enough.

Saturday, January 25, 1930. Jotted down the outline for "the forestation bulletin" for the southern pine region, while Chris sang in the kitchen.

Evidently the "jotting" was preliminary and informal. The next identifiable references are:

Friday, June 6, 1930. Took leave in the afternoon to stay with Don and Pat, while Chris went to Mrs. Bond's bridge lunch. I drew up the outline of my bulletin and Chris drew second prize, six bits.

Saturday, June 7, 1930. Talked over the bulletin outline with Demmie.

Thursday, June 12, 1930.…sent outline of bulletin to Washington and summarized references and correspondence necessary in working up the text.

Charles Delaney, Sr., Paul V. Siggers, Luther Delaney, W.R. Hine, and N.D. Canterbury evaluating nursery seedlings at the LA State Nursery at Woodworth.

It is noteworthy and characteristic of the epoch, that I could and did summarize in one Saturday morning the pertinent literature and the unpublished material available for and necessary to documentation of this bulletin. (When I wrote its sequel, Agriculture Monograph 18, a couple of decades later, I abstracted more than 2,000 publications and reports, a job that took well over a man-year.) Of course, I picked up more as writing progressed. I cited more than 100 publications in the finished manuscript. The number seemed excessive to the Washington Office, which arbitrarily crossed some of them out; the "lit.cit." in the printed version consists of exactly 40 items. A few authors whose findings were on this account, incorporated without credit, wrote protests to the Washington Office, which ordered *me* to write the necessary apologies!

Perhaps Washington was slow to comment on the outline submitted in June 1930. Also, much routine work on going studies and a multitude of special assignments and odd jobs intervened. My official diary for December 1930 mentions resumption of work on the bulletin manuscript. The next notes concerning it in my personal diary were:

Saturday, January 3, 1931. Shut my door and wrote bulletin manuscript all morning. Manuscript not much good, but at least it is under way.

Friday, January 16, 1931. Got nothing done, except to discard all my bulletin text to date and start fresh.

Tuesday, June 2, 1931…Afternoon on computations and bulletin text. Invited Miss Bergland into my office to type photograph cards in the afternoon; an excellent scheme, as it kept visitors out and kept us both working steadily.

Then came a gap. I was assigned the job of indexing all the Station photographs, some 1,500 in number as I recall, and did so. (Betty Bergland typed the 3 by 5 index cards, including cross-reference cards. These cards were all thrown away in

June 1964 to save drawer space in the Station Library. This was not as bad as it sounds; most of the photographs had been thrown away years before.) After that, I was detached from Forestation Project work to write the South Pasture Report for use in Demmon's fire bulletin. My next diary entry pertinent to my own forestation bulletin was:

Saturday, January 30, 1932. Back to work on my bulletin, untouched since last July. Merely refamiliarized myself with the material, but it's good to be back.

During July and August 1932, Jean Kerr, who was then the Service's editor, was detailed to the Station to give us a lift with technical writing. On August 12 my diary recorded:

A good session with Miss Kerr on my 'one-third' bulletin; she's blue-pencilled it remarkably little considering it is the roughest of rough drafts and is most encouraging in her comments on its sense and style.

Then my assignment in connection with that notable command-performance publication, the Copeland Report, brought the bulletin to a full stop.

By January 11, 1933, I was desperate. The daughter of a next-door neighbor, a recent business-school graduate (and for many years afterwards, a top-flight executive secretary with Sears Roebuck), was looking for a job. (This was during the Depression.) On January 13, I arranged with her to take the remaining two-thirds of the bulletin (introduction and nursery and planting chapters) in shorthand and type it on my typewriter in half-page width, double-spaced, in elite type, at five cents a half page. I wanted it in this half-page form (lefthand half only) for correction and amendment.

I spent my time in the office the next few days digging out and collating the information needed for this process. I dictated to Yvonne at home at night and she transcribed the next day. In *20 calendar days* from the start, we had the remaining two-thirds of the bulletin done; this in contrast to the *24 months* required to write the first third under normal office conditions. Of course, the draft that we had was rough and incomplete, but it was something definite on which to work. I had to pay Yvonne out of my own pocket, of course, but it was worth it.

Between April 29 and June 8, I revised the dictated draft and Ruth Marshall typed the revision; this was official, not at my expense. On or shortly after June 8, we sent an original and one carbon of the (official) rough draft to Washington for advisory comments and as a prelude to filling certain gaps from files (particularly W.R. Mattoon's on early work at Summerville, South Carolina) available only in Washington. During this period, what with the strain of technical work, some serious dental trouble and anxiety arising from the Depression, I developed the first symptoms of an acute reversed paristalsis that reached a climax when I was driving north a little later on leave and that nearly ruined our first family vacation in our first car. Bulletin 492 was beginning to hurt.

After I had recovered from this illness, I interrupted my vacation and spent about a week in Washington, where I got the greater part of the bulletin data I wanted and some rather spurious encouragement from Ed Munns and Jean Kerr, but no decisions on the main points at issue.

Between August 9 and September 18, 1933, I re-revised enough of the bulletin to get typing started on the final draft to be submitted for publication. By this time, Washington had set an absolute deadline, October 1, 1933, for receipt of the final draft, but as October 1 was a Sunday, we allowed ourselves one day's grace. Meeting that deadline was strenuous work. For example:

Sunday, September 17, 1933. A full and successful day. Up before 6 and wrote for nearly an hour, revising the section on seed testing. Then for a a swim…before breakfast. After breakfast, to the office and cleared up an immense amount of work and rearranged several jobs so that I could have everything ready for Ruth to start typing in the morning.

Between September 17 and September 26, Ruth and I trod on each other's heels, so to speak, typing and revising. Yvonne did some more typing for me at the last minute September 29, (but this was at Station expense), to help meet the deadline.

Saturday, September 30, 1933. Got the bulletin off to Washington on schedule time, thanks in great part to excellent teamwork by the girls. At one time this morning, I had six girls and two men working for me, including Demmie himself, who completed a table. Mailed one copy myself about 2:30, registered, with a request for a return receipt.

Wednesday, October 4, 1933. The return receipt from the registered copy of my bulletin came back, post- marked 3:00 p.m., October 2. We got it to Washington on time.

Thursday, October 5, 1933. A curt acknowledgment of my bulletin from Ed.

And that was the last I heard of this, my first major Government Printing Office publication, for 9 months. I was pretty happy about it. My personal diary for October 17 contains the entry:

Attempt to decide what to do about the situation involved in my sending the bulletin manuscript to Washington with tables imperfect or incomplete…told Chris all about the whole wretched mess of publications before we went to bed and lay awake thinking about it after that.

Friday, October 20, 1933…."recomputation of bulletin tables at the office."

I seem to have made no further diary entries, official or personal, concerning the bulletin until about the end of June 1934, when I was ordered by wire to report to Washington to go over the manuscript with the editor, Jean Kerr.

That was a miserable trip. The only mitigating circumstances were a fine fireworks display on the Mall on July 4, seeing William Powell and Myrna Loy twice in "The Thin Man" and meeting Roy Chapman's wife for the first time. I was away from home on Chris's and my 10th wedding anniversary. Washington was hotter than New Orleans; the temperature neared or hit 100° every day of the 2 weeks I was there and was 101° in the Union Depot at midnight the night I started back to New Orleans. I am sure, too, by process of elimination, that this was the occasion on which Cap Eldredge, who was acting Director, indulged his devilish sense of humor to the extent of sending me to Washington on a $3.00 per diem (the cheapest hotel room I could get was $3.50), though he himself was touring the small towns of the South on a $5.00 per diem in connection with the Forest Survey. Not exactly the ideal ecological niche in which to do really fine writing.

But the human environment was worse than the physical.

The original wrapper of the registered ribbon copy of the manuscript and the unopened carbon copies sent a few days later by ordinary mail, were on a table in Ed's office in July 1934. Remembering our frantic efforts to meet the deadline the previous fall, I wrote the transmittal date, September 30, 1933 with my finger in the dust that had settled on the wrapping paper during the intervening 9 months.

Ed told me that the manuscript was the worst his office had ever received and said he doubted whether 200 copies of the finished work would ever be called for. He also changed the title from "Artificial regeneration with the southern pines to Artificial regeneration in the Southern Pine Region" because an appendix listed several dozen exotic pines that had failed in the South. Later, without restoring the original title, he deleted that appendix and we are still boldly criticized for not warning people (the St. Joe Paper Company, for example) that

Pinus radiata and other species that require a "Mediterranian" climate are ill adapted to the Gulf Station.

The heat wave had given Jean Kerr insomnia and the good nature that had marked her visit to New Orleans in 1932 was no longer of evidence. She blue-penciled the manuscript to a running fire of sarcastic comment. (She was, to my secret amusement, especially severe on some of the bits she had herself inserted in the seed chapter in 1932 and undeservedly so, I think, for she was an excellent writer.) She and I put in a good deal of overtime at the office and worked long hours alone almost every night, with next to no clothes on because of the heat in my cheap hotel. We finally got the job done. I was glad to get away.

The summary of my official diary for June 1935 contains the following:

> *Inserted final corrections in manuscript of Technical Bulletin 'Artificial reforestation in the Southern Pine Region' in the light of comments by other bureaus, to permit its going to press during fiscal year 1935.*

I read, corrected and approved the galley proof September 4-6, 1935. My official diary for Friday, October 25, 1935, says:

> *...spent the entire day correcting page proof of the forestation bulletin—114 pages. One very bad error introduced in cut-title and several minor errors, but proof as a whole very good and bulletin as a whole better in tone and appearance than I had dared hope. Great relief to get it past this stage.*

We returned the proof to Washington, with corrections the next day.

For politic reasons, I have no doubt my official diary omitted mention of one particular correction.

The original text had included a formula for converting the weight, in grams, of a sample of seeds into number of seeds per pound. It read $\frac{X}{Y} = \frac{4536}{Z}$, in which X represented the number of seeds per pound (to be determined), Y the number of seeds in the sample and Z, the weight of the sample in grams. The formula had been printed correctly in the galley proof, and I had approved it. In the page proof, however, to my consternation, the portion "X divided by Y" had been changed to "X times Y!"

Miss Kerr was not mathematically inclined; in fact, I believe she had taught Greek for 9 years or so, before turning editor. It seems that someone in the Washington Office, who shall be nameless, had persuaded her that the bulletin was addressed principally to State Foresters and that the State Foresters in the South (including, if you please, such men as Holmes of North Carolina and Siecke of Texas) were mostly ignorant political appointees, incapable of understanding complicated technical writing. In all innocence, she had changed "X/Y" to "X.Y" because she thought the latter would be easier for State Foresters to understand!

Miss Kerr's version of the formula had remarkable properties. According to it, if coconuts weighed a pound apiece, there would automatically be 43,560,000 coconuts to the pound. We worked this problem out and sent it to the Washington Office with the suggestion that, for the honor of the Department, they restore the formula to the form approved in the galley proof. We finally compromised on a specialized version involving no unknowns and applicable only to samples of 1,000 seeds each and this appeared in the bulletin as issued. The Government Printing Office charged author's correction for resetting the type and the Washington Office wrote us an unpleasant letter about this extra item of cost.

The preface to my personal journal for 1936 includes the statement, "My first big bulletin...., which I started in 1931, is somewhere in the Government Printing Office." U.S. Department Agriculture Tech. Bul. 492, "Artificial reforestation in the Southern Pine Region", although dated November 1935, actually came off the press in January 1936, 11 years and 3 months after my arrival at the Station as a Temporary Field Assistant. I saw my first copy of it in the Regional Office in Atlanta during the Annual Meeting of the Society of American Foresters held in that city and found 50 "author's copies" waiting for me when I returned to New Orleans on February 7 via Thomasville, Georgia, Lake City, Florida, and the Ocala National Forest.

The only further mention of this bulletin in my diary for many, many years is:

> *February 13, 1936. A letter from Washington would seem to indicate that my bulletin is almost out of print already.*

It was too. Ed Munns' prediction that it would be hard to move 200 copies proved wide of the mark. The first printing, if I remember correctly, was 3,500 copies and only a few weeks after the bulletin appeared, the Washington Office asked for my 50 author's copies back, to answer urgent requests. We sent 40 of them—I had already given away 10—transmitting them over Demmon's signature.

Demmie took this opportunity to twit the Washington Office gently for having misjudged the merits of the work and Ed Munns replied plaintively that this was unfair; a lot of the demand had come from the Soil Conservation Service and could not possibly have been predicted at the time the manuscript was received. This seemed to us at the Station a rather thin excuse, the humor of which compensated me a little for the emotional wear and tear of authorship. Only a little, however; it was many months before I could bring myself to read the finished work.

The bad taste that the production of "492" had left in my mouth gradually passed away. I am not ashamed of the publication itself; for its time and considering the circumstances under which it was written, it was a respectable achievement. It became virtually the bible of the CCC

Wakeley's Tech. Bulletin 492 provided the guidelines for the CCC reforestation efforts during the Depression. It was expanded with additional information and published in 1954 as "Planting the Southern Pines." Wakeley's research was so thorough that his guidelines have become the established practices for southern pine reforestation.

planting program in the South and was reprinted to meet the continuing demand for this purpose. We also received numbers of compliments on it from abroad.

What finally took all the sting out of authorship, however, was an episode in 1937 or thereabouts. Enroute home on a Sunday from some trip, I stopped by to see the then relatively new (but now long since abandoned) Alabama State Forest Nursery between Livingston and York. It was on rather poor soil. The nurseryman, Curtis Merchant, was a local farmer, not a professional forester like Read in DeRidder and was running the nursery with little technical guidance from Montgomery. He was doing a good job, however, and I spent a pleasant hour exchanging information and taking photographs and notes before it was time for him to take his wife to church.

As church time approached, I took my leave but stopped on the way to the car to photograph a fine rambler rose growing on the nursery fence. I offered Mr. Merchant a print of the photograph in the event it came out well and got my notebook out again to write down his rural mail address.

He got out his notebook too and asked for my own name and address, explaining that he was very poor at catching names. When I spelled my name out for him, he suddenly got very red in the face, snatched off his hat and stammered, "Why... why...why...you 're the man who wrote *the bulletin*!

I have carried this account of Bulletin 492 to its conclusion, far beyond the end of the Second Era, to get the story down all in one piece. The space devoted to the story is, of course,

part of my personal bias inherent in this history. I think the documentation is important, however. It re-creates a "feel" and it lays the foundation for a favorite thesis of mine: Technical writing need not and should not be as harrowing a job as it too often is. It should be fun. The cold fact remains that the second half of the Second Era itself—that is, from January 1931 to the summer and fall of 1933—became increasingly trying to me personally as my gaily undertaken efforts to write a bulletin turned more and more sour.

DEPRESSION AND SUSPENSE

I was the chief sufferer insofar as Bulletin 492 was concerned, but the bulletin was not my only source of distress toward the end of the Second Era. Despite our benefits and the Station's expansion under the McNary-McSweeney Act of 1928, all of us on the staff ended the era under considerable difficulties and in greater trepidation. These grew out of the Depression that started with the Stock Market crash of 1929 and reached a climax with the Bank Holiday of 1933.

Historians, novelists, economists, and sociologists have written innumerable books about the Depression. Its causes, effects and chances of duplication are still fruitful sources of debate but are of no moment here. For the purposes of this history, it seems to me that the following excerpts from my personal journal tell the story well enough. This then, was the atmosphere in which we conducted our research as the Era of Expansion and Recognition drew to a close.

Tuesday, October 27, 1931. J.K. (Johnson) says the Great Southern is putting in no nursery next year. As he expresses it, they're "staying mighty close to shore."

One of our most powerful industrial cooperators, and in many ways the best, was already hard hit. The company sold out in the mid-Thirties to Gaylord Container Corporation, which did not resume planting till 1939 or thereabouts.

Sunday, April 10, 1932. On one page of this morning's paper, President Hoover agrees to an 11% reduction in federal salaries and on another, he urges each of us (including, presumably, federal employees) to buy now the car he has been planning on.

Wednesday, June 1, 1932. The latest "economy" move seems to be to abolish all annual leave for fiscal year 1933.

Thursday, June 23, 1932. Entered on annual leave; we're limited to 7-1/2 days and must take it by June 30.

Friday, July 15, 1932. Disquieting news at the office; my per diem set at only $3.00 per day; our pay delayed until nearly the end of the month... and, worst of all, rumor that we may have to take our furloughs on Saturdays instead of all at once.

The "furloughs" were 11 percent of all working days in the year. As a means of recompensing us for the 11-percent cut in pay, we don't have to work on these days. But if they had to be taken piecemeal, on Saturdays, we couldn't use them for trips or other real vacations.

Friday, March 3, 1933. The banks have "frozen" 95% of every account, apparently for an indefinite period. Wish I'd paid my bills in advance this month.

My particular bank, the Interstate Trust and Banking Company, at the corner of Canal and Camp, went into receivership. We had our checking account and four savings accounts in it. We finally got the last of our deposits back, without interest, some time after 1952.

Monday, March 6, 1933. A heady excitement in our work. The banks are closed all over the United States for 4 days and there is much talk of scrip. We have our salary checks but can't cash them and several of us are postponing field trips for lack of funds. (Tonight's paper says Ex-President Hoover has been delayed on his return to California by lack of funds too.)

Hoover's term of office as President had ended March 4 with Franklin D. Roosevelt's inauguration.

Tuesday, March 7, 1933. Spent more than an hour getting an identification signature from the Interstate on my salary check and getting it cashed at the Federal Reserve, among a lot of pensioners, while knots of surly-looking, unprepossessing men looked on now and then from the sidewalks.

Some of the staff were cursed roundly by these groups and one at least reported being threatened with violence.

Saturday, March 11, 1933 ... crew of "unemployed" grubbing stumps along the highway and afraid to talk lest they lose their jobs...

... Roosevelt's plan to reduce salaries and then adjust them every 6 months in accordance with living cost...

To reduce salaries still more below those already reduced 11 percent. The stump-grubbers were along the highway to Bogalusa, where I had gone on previously scheduled fieldwork shortly after cashing my month's check at the Federal Reserve Bank.

Saturday, March 18, 1933. Informed our furlough, already deducted for, will be cancelled if not taken by April 1. Am saying nothing to Chris.

March 18, 1933, was my thirty-first birthday and the above announcement was not a pleasant birthday gift. We were planning to use the furlough in June for our first trip north by car, with our three children, to attend our tenth class reunion at Cornell. The furlough was not cancelled as of April 1, after all, but the thought of keeping still about it, while Chris and the two older children planned every detail of the journey, combined with the strain of a rush job on Bulletin 492 to bring on the illness that incapacitated me on the trip.

Monday, April 24, 1933. Lot of panicky talk about reduction or abandonment of all agricultural research, including forest research, but I believe Roosevelt has too much sense for that, and besides, Mr. Clapp is on deck.

Earl Clapp was at that time Assistant Chief of the U.S. Forest Service, in Charge of Research.

Monday, May 1, 1933. Staff meeting, with encouraging word from Washington about the continuation of our work.

But next:

Thursday, July 6, 1933. (In Washington) Ed Munns. . .very gloomy about present and impending cuts in research funds. Even Mr. Clapp pretty sober.

Saturday, September 2, 1933. Find that my travel from now till June 30 is limited to $33.50.

This September 2 allotment worked out to a total of $3.72 a month, for transportation and expenses combined, to keep the field work of the Regeneration Project going in the Station's then territory of eight States, from South Carolina to Arkansas and Texas.

The other Projects, with the exception probably of the Forest Survey, were no better off. We were severely straitened financially, and practically bankrupt in spirit. As far as we could tell, our livelihood and our program were both in imminent danger of being demolished. What money we had individually had, and none of us had had much, was frozen in the bank and with many millions of people unemployed, the prospect of our getting other work was practically nil.

This makes the best of all places to terminate this biased history. The motion picture industry established the precedent years ago in a serial called "The Perils of Pauline." Each episode ended with Silent Actress Pearl White bound hand and foot to a railroad track or hanging by her fingertips over a cliff, and I'll leave the Southern Station hanging over a cliff in the same way.

-Finis-

SIGNIFICANCE OF WAKELEY'S AND HIS COLLEAGUES' CONTRIBUTIONS

With only a handful of professional foresters, little technical support, and primitive working conditions, early forest research in the South made enormous contributions to the economic and social well being of the region. The researchers developed reforestation techniques, studied and began to understand the role of fire in forests, began surveys of the southern forests that led to development and expansion of forest industries, studied important insect and disease pests and learned how to manage them. They also developed an understanding of the importance of the use of statistical design and the value of tree improvement, provided methodologies to control soil erosion, and improved the efficiency of producing forest products.

Three very significant contributions of these pioneers in the Southern Station Experimental Forest made forestry a leader in the economic development of the South. First was the Southern Forest Survey. Planning for this project began in 1929 and I.F. 'Cap' Eldredge was assigned the task of carrying it out in 1932. The survey was more than a gigantic timber cruise. As important as data on total wood volume by individual tree species, was information on industrial use, mortality, and net growth. For the first time each State knew the ratio of growth to drain. Industry for the first time had factual data on which to make decisions about mill locations.

Conducting the survey was a massive undertaking. A system was formulated where compass lines ran 10 miles apart across each State from Tennessee southward to the tip of Florida. At every 660 feet on these lines, plots were established and a great deal of information was taken. Fortunately for the Southern Research Station, many of the best timber men in the South were available to work on the survey because of the Great Depression. The survey started at the Atlantic Coast and ended in the prairies of Texas. Remarkably, the field effort was completed in 4 years, although analysis and publication of data took longer. For this first time, regional and national leaders had factual data on the extent, location, and condition of the southern forest.

The second major accomplishment was the 1929 publication of "Volume, yield, and stand tables for second-growth southern pines" (U.S. Department of Agriculture Forest Service 1929). Known as Miscellaneous Publication 50, the tables allowed decisionmakers to estimate with reasonable confidence the potential growth and economic benefits of the southern forest. This was another massive

undertaking. Crews went across the South selecting stands, felling trees, and making measurements. For decades, the pocket sized Miscellaneous Pub 50 was the standard for estimating growth and yield of pine stands. Copies became worn and tattered, but highly prized. Due to popular demand the publication was reprinted in 1976, after many more modern and scientifically based growth and yield models became available.

Publication of Wakeley's (1954) "Planting the Southern Pines" represents the third major accomplishment of this early group of researchers. This document, and an earlier version (Wakeley 1935), made possible "dibble-ready" projects the Civilian Conservation Corps used to demonstrate the feasibility of large-scale reforestation. The technology and methodology outlined in Wakeley's book enabled the states and private forest landowners to rapidly expand seedling production and planting in response to the Soil Bank Program of the early 1960s. "Planting the Southern Pines" became basis for nursery production and plantation establishment across the South and is likely the most cited publication of the Southern Forest Experiment Station.

Together, the forest survey, "Miscellaneous Publication 50", and "Planting the Southern Pines" provided the basis for projecting the resource supply and convincing bankers and

A photo of Phil Wakeley taken in 1962 late in his career. At this time he had developed regional, national, and international recognition for his contributions to the restoration of the South's forests.

industrialists to invest billions to expand the pulp and paper, lumber and plywood industries throughout the region.

How did these early research professionals with limited resources convert decimated forest land into a tremendous economic resource in a relatively short period of time? Dedication, cooperation, and teamwork were characteristics of the early research program. Wakeley and his colleagues were fortunate to be associated to two visionary timberland owners: Henry H. Hardtner of Urania Lumber Company and Col. William Sullivan of Great Southern Lumber Company who provided practical ideas as well as resources to support research. Not only did

Wakeley and his associates support each other's efforts, they developed excellent relationships with scientists in universities and other agencies, and foresters in forest industry and State organizations that were dedicated to solving problems common to all organizations.

In < 25 years, these pioneer researchers provided the basic management guidelines that resulted in great progress being made in the restoration of the South's forest lands. In more recent decades, research has largely refined and filled in gaps of this knowledge. Research continues to build on the strong scientific understanding provided by these early researchers. As a result, our restored southern forest lands are now the primary economic resource in most all southern States.

The South's forests had been so thoroughly harvested that little regeneration was occurring in the early 1920s when Wakeley and his associates began to develop reforestation and other forestry technology. Their research was very successful—such that during their careers, millions of acres of southern forests were restored and these forests were becoming the economic mainstay of the Southern United States.

LITERATURE CITED

Ashe, W.W. 1915. Loblolly or North Carolina pine. Bulletin 24. Raleigh, NC: North Carolina Geological and Economic Survey. 176 p.

Barnett, J.P. 2004. Southern forest resource conditions and management practices from 1900–1950. In: Rauscher, H. Michael; Johnsen, Kurt, eds. Southern Forest Science: Past, Present, and Future. Gen. Tech. Rep. SRS-75. Asheville, NC: U.S. Department of Agriculture, Forest Service, Southern Research Station: 15-22.

Barnett, J.P.; Vozzo, J.A. 1985. Viability and vigor of slash and shortleaf pine seeds after 50 years of storage. Forest Science. 31: 316-320.

Campbell, T.E. 1976. The nation's oldest industrial direct seeding. Forests & People. 26(3): 22-24.

Chapman, H.H. 1922. A new hybrid pine (*Pinus palustris* x *Pinus taeda*). Journal of Forestry. 20: 729-734.

Chapman, H.H. 1923. The recovery and growth of loblolly pine after suppression. Journal of Forestry. 21: 709-711.

Chapman, H.H. 1926. Factors determining natural reproduction of longleaf pine on cutover lands in LaSalle Parish, Louisiana. Bull. 16. New Haven, CT: Yale University School of Forestry. 44 p.

Goodyear, C.W. 1950. Bogalusa. Buffalo, NY: C.W. Goodyear. 208 p.

Heyward, F. 1963. Col. W.H. Sullivan—Paul Bunyan of Louisiana Forestry. Forests & People. 13(1): 20.

Kerr, E. 1958. History of forestry in Louisiana. Baton Rouge, LA: Louisiana Forestry Commission, Office of the State Forester. 55 p.

Mattoon, W.R. 1922. Longleaf pine. Bulletin 1061. Washington, DC: U.S. Department of Agriculture. 50 p.

Maunder, E. 1963. Henry Hardtner signs the first reforestation contract. Forests & People. 13(1): 56-57, 124-125.

Putnam, J.A.; Bull, H. 1932. The trees of the bottomlands of the Mississippi River Delta Region. Occasional Paper 27. New Orleans: U.S. Department of Agriculture, Forest Service, Southern Forest Experiment Station. 207 p.

Schumacher, F.X.; Chapman, R.A. 1942. Sampling methods in forestry and range management. Bulletin 7. Durham, NC: Duke University, School of Forestry. 213 p.

U.S. Department of Agriculture. 1929. Volume, yield, and stand tables for second-growth southern pines. Misc. Publ. 50. Washington, DC: U.S. Department of Agriculture, Forest Service. 202 p.

Wahlenberg, W.G. 1946. Longleaf pine: its use, ecology, regeneration, protection, growth and management. Washington, DC: Charles Lathrop Pack Forestry Foundation. 429 p.

Wahlenberg, W.G. 1960. Loblolly pine: its, use, ecology, regeneration, protection, growth and management. Durham, NC: Duke University, School of Forestry. 603 p.

Wakeley, P.C. 1935. Artificial reforestation in the southern pine region. Tech. Bulletin 492. Washington, DC: U.S. Department of Agriculture, Forest Service. 115 p.

Wakeley, P.C. 1944. Geographic seed source of loblolly pine seed. Journal of Forestry. 42: 23-33.

Wakeley, P.C. 1954. Planting the southern pines. Agric. Monograph 18. Washington, DC: U.S. Department of Agriculture, Forest Service. 233 p.

Wakeley, P.C.; Barnett, J.P. 1968. Viability of slash and shortleaf pine seed stored for 35 years. Journal of Forestry. 66: 840-841.

Wheeler, P.R. 1963. The coming of forest research. Forests & People. 13(1): 66-67, 96, 98-101, 110-111.

White, R.R. 1961. Austin Cary, the father of southern forestry. Forest History. 5: 2-5.

Williston, H.L. 1988. The Yazoo-Little Tallahatchie Flood Prevention Project: a history of the Forest Service's role. Forestry Report R8-FR8. Atlanta, GA: U.S. Department of Agriculture, Forest Service, Southern Region. 63 p.